W9-ABR-716

MANUEL DE FALLA AND SPANISH MUSIC

MANUEL DE FALLA
AND
SPANISH MUSIC

By J. B. Trend

NEW YORK
ALFRED · A · KNOPF
MCMXXXIV

To

A. H. P. and M. P.

This book is in no sense an interview. Neither is it a panegyric. Its object is to give an account of the work of a contemporary composer — to understand his intentions, describe his methods and point out his achievements. Falla once wrote that music is not made to be understood, but to be experienced, felt; and in conversation his most frequent description of an interpreter or a critic is that he " understands my intentions " — or does not.

These pages, then, deal not with the man, but with his music, as far as I can understand his intentions and can put them into words. They must not be taken as the composer's own account of himself, though in the two chapters devoted to the origins of the Spanish style I have availed myself of such explanation of technical problems as he has published, over his own signature and in Spanish. Statements reported to have been made to interviewers have been rejected, for such statements are commonly expressed in vague, ready-made phrases of French origin, foreign to the composer's habitual directness and individuality of expression, whether in words or music.

Though part of the book is concerned with Spanish folk-song and the origins of the so-called

" Spanish idiom," Falla is not a composer to whom arguments against the use of folk-tunes can be applied; for, with the exception of his *Seven Spanish Songs* and the short phrases which characterize the miller and his wife in *The Three-Cornered Hat*, he has hardly used folk-tunes at all, and his treatment of the rhythms of the dance and the harmonic effects of the guitar has an originality which only those who know them in their usual form can properly appreciate.

Falla's music gives everyone the chance of becoming acquainted with the tendencies of contemporary composers. His methods sometimes recall those of Stravinsky, Bartók, Honegger or Vaughan Williams; but his music is more widely accessible and the clearness of his outlines and the vigour of his rhythms never leave his intentions for a moment in doubt. He frankly faces the fact " that music is made up in the first instance of physical sounds," but the forced insincerity of the Parisian " Armistice " school has never touched him.

The book begins with certain general considerations on Spanish music: the " Spanish style," the work of Pedrell, and the so-called " renaissance " of Spanish music — all of which are intended to help towards an understanding of Falla's position in the musical world of today. Some readers may find the personal impressions of Chapter III more to their taste or the descriptions of individual works with the numerous musical

examples which the Publisher has so generously al-
lowed. Others may be frightened at the number of
words in Spanish (or even in Arabic) which have been
used from time to time, though all of them have been
translated to the best of my ability into everyday English and have only been used to make the point clearer
than it would have been without them. For the pages
which follow have all been written in the hope that
they may lead others besides myself to the enjoyment
of musical experiences which (when I look back on
them) have been more intense than those derived
from any other contemporary music.

J. B. T.

Barrington, Cambridge
7 June, 1929

CONTENTS

INTRODUCTION

I

Towards the end of the nineteenth century a change came over the outlook of the more alert composers in Europe. Its effects were felt in Spain, no less than in England, France, Russia, Hungary, and other countries. It has been called the " renaissance," though the employment of that word tends to add to the confusion of thought caused by its use in other connexions. The term " renaissance " has been applied to other periods in the history of music: to the music of " renaissance times," for instance — Josquin des Prés, Morales, Lasso, Byrd, Victoria, and the other sixteenth century masters; and again (mistakenly) to the changes in technique which accompanied the establishment of opera, when the " renaissance " style in the other arts was already giving place to the baroque.

What writers mean when they speak of the renaissance of music in modern times is not a " rebirth," but *a getting down to facts*. The facts of musical experience have to be excavated and exposed to view before any rebirth can take place; indeed " rebirth " is the last stage in the process, for it must be preceded by the reform which comes from a study of the facts. Spengler would claim that no art of any greatness has ever been " reborn ": the process glibly described as " renaissance " is one in which " an eye really free from prepossessions would have seen another art being born in another landscape to express another humanity." Then of course comes a counter-reform, to assert the authority of the older, orthodox view against the adventurous inquiry of the new. The recent musical renaissance in various countries has been brought about by adventurous exploration. By getting down to the facts and exposing to view once more the musical traditions of those countries, it is free in spirit, — a protest against any form of dictatorship, whether Latin or German. It is free no less in England, where culture is a bridge between the Latin and the Teutonic, than it is in Spain, which, deeply Romanized as it was, owes many of its peculiarities to the fact that it too was a bridge for seven hundred years between a Latin civilization and the civilization of Islam.

II

On a primitive Iberian and Celtic foundation, at the edges of which had fallen a sprinkling of Phœnicians, "Tartessians," and Greeks, were laid successive strata of Roman and Visigothic (i.e., Germanic) influence; but the Arab and Berber invasion of 711 led to the opening up of Spain to influences from the middle East — from Persia and India as well as from those countries in the near East where the civilization encountered by the Arabs had still been to a large extent that of hellenistic Greece.

One of the earliest records we have of music in Spain — music, that is, as an *art* — is the singing of Ziryâb, a Persian, who came from Baghdad in the ninth century and settled at Córdoba, where he founded a celebrated school of singing. The earliest pictorial representations of musical performances in Spain belong to the same period, and the musicians depicted on ivory caskets made at Córdoba in the tenth century can be related both in the form of their instruments and the manner of their dress to the musicians whom we know (from coins) were playing in Baghdad about the same time.

Spain, as we know it today, seems to be pre-eminently a country of the dance, and no interpreter of Spanish music can make us feel its full beauty or vitality unless he feel those vital dance-rhythms within himself. Spanish dance-rhythms, especially in southern Spain, may be attributed with a considerable degree of probability to an Islamic, African source; but there are melodies which have an earlier, eastern origin, although their date of arrival in the Peninsula is considerably later, having been brought by gipsies, who are first heard of in Spain in 1442. Whether the gipsies were the inventors of the melodies they brought, or (as is more probable) only the transmitters of melodies they had picked up on their wanderings or in their new home in Spain, they gradually became — with their roving habits and exaggerated style of performance — the typical musicians of the people, more especially after the last of the Moriscos (the Moorish converts to Christianity) were expelled from Spain, about 1620.

Yet the " facts " of a country's music are not, entirely and exclusively, folk-song and folk-dance, or the melodic and rhythmic features peculiar to them. The facts include also the tradition of cultivated music, which, in Spain, may be taken to mean Mozarabic chant, the troubadour tunes of Alfonso the Sage, the earlier secular pieces for three and four voices, the sixteenth-century lute-music, the church-music of Morales and Victoria, and the Spanish harpsichord music of Domenico Scarlatti. And the " renaissance " of music, in Spain as elsewhere, in all extensions of the word and in all stages of the process (excavation, reform, and then — perhaps — rebirth), depends on cultivated music no less than on music of a less sophisticated origin.

III

If Manuel de Falla is to be described as a child of the Spanish musical renaissance, we must consider, not whether we can find traces in his work of all the stages of his country's musical culture, but whether he is the heir to that culture and has entered into his inheritance. For to us, men and women of today, it is

xvi

surely not extravagant to imagine that the past has existed mainly for our benefit, to spare or spoil as we may; just as we exist (if we create anything) not for ourselves or only for our own age, but also for the future. Every real creative artist must have felt, at certain moments, that all the labour of the past has been for him, has been leading up to him and has been a preparation for his own work; and that it has fallen to him, and him only, to put the crown upon it — if he can! . . . It is a dream, of course, and it ends in disillusion:

> Que toda la vida es sueño,
> y los sueños sueño son.

For the few who do crown the work of their predecessors, and at the same time open the way for those who come after, are often unconscious of what they do; not realizing that the thing that comes nearest to them, the thing on which they have set their heart or which has always been the goal of their ambition, may be at the same time the keystone of the arch, the support of all future construction.

The keystone of the arch upon which modern Spanish music rests is the work of Felipe Pedrell.

MANUEL DE FALLA AND SPANISH MUSIC

CHAPTER I

PEDRELL

It is curious to observe that even in the hands of genuine Spanish composers: Albéniz, Granados, Turina, and Falla, the only types of music which sound " Spanish " to a non-Spanish audience are those which recall the more obvious songs and dances of Andalucía or the *jota* of Navarre; and there are even Spanish people who hold the same opinion. Falla (they sometimes say) is always inclined to write " French " (i.e., foreign, un-Spanish) music, and becomes denationalized and unintelligible when he abandons the Andaluz manner, as he has done since *The Puppet-Show* and the Harpsichord Concerto.

At that rate the music of Pedrell, on the few occasions on which it has ever been played — at Venice under Tebaldini, in Paris under Charles Bordes, in Germany and in Holland, in Barcelona and Buenos Aires — must have sounded so remote from everyday musical experience as to make little or no impression on the hearers; or, at most, to give a certain impression of post-Wagnerian harmony, but no impression at all of its melodic wealth and variety.

Yet Pedrell was not only a musical antiquary, who collected folk-songs, copied manuscripts, and

3

reconstructed ancient music by scoring it from the separate voice-parts — the untiring researcher who went back to the facts of Spanish musical tradition and placed them within the reach of living Spanish composers. He was himself a good composer, in some ways a great composer. "They have never done me justice," he said to Falla, not long before his death, "either in Catalonia or in the rest of Spain. They have constantly tried to belittle me, saying that I was a great critic, or a great historian, but not a good composer. It's not true! I *am* a good composer! I don't want respect for my years, but for my work. Let them hear it and study it; they will be able to judge me then!"

This estimate of Pedrell is true, though it is his own estimate of himself. He was not a good critic, because, although he had good judgment, he was unable to express it without entering into controversy; and he was not a good historian, because his learning, immense though it was, could never be reduced to order or put on paper. His proper means of expression was music, and the works for which he should be chiefly remembered are his original compositions: the two operas, *Los Pirineos* and *La Celestina,* and the great choral ballad *El Comte Arnau;* together with his complete edition of Victoria and Cabezón, his collections of old Spanish church-music and old Spanish theatre-music, and his *Cancionero,* a collection of traditional songs from all parts of Spain. This last was the key to his whole life's work.

Besides being a good composer, Pedrell was also a good teacher. " Pedrell," Falla has written,[1] " was a master in the highest sense of the word, for both by precept and example he showed Spanish musicians where their road lay and led them along it himself. . . . Some of those who were his pupils have let it be understood that they did not get much benefit from his lessons. It may have been that they did not know how to profit by them, or that they tried to obtain from them something that was definitely opposed to the strong æsthetic convictions of the master. Or, again, it may be that they went to him without the technical preparation necessary to every student who goes to a great artist for advice. But, whatever the cause," he adds, " I for my part am able to affirm that I owe to the teaching of Pedrell, and to the powerful stimulus exerted on me by his music, that artistic direction which is indispensable to every well-intentioned apprentice."

Pedrell's editions of old Spanish music, important as they are, played only a small part in the salutary influence which he exercised over Spanish musicians.

[1] *Felipe Pedrell: 1841–1922* (Barcelona, 1923). This study first appeared in French, in the *Revue Musicale;* but in this, as in all other cases, I have preferred to go back to the original Spanish.

For a copy of this rare pamphlet, as well as a gift of the score of *El Comte Arnau,* I am indebted to a good friend to both Pedrell and Falla: Don Juan Gisbert, of Barcelona.

Falla, who (as we have seen) felt the stimulus and accepted the guidance of Pedrell's own compositions, roundly declares that they alone would have been enough to cause the rebirth of Spanish music; although more important still were the personal influence of the master himself, and his endeavours to make the classics of Spanish music more generally known to students. These activities greatly increased the effects wrought by his own music and fortified it in its action. He did not, as a rule, reproduce his historical knowledge directly in his compositions; but he strove, by its help, to make his music reflect such valuable features as were to be found in the musical tradition of his own country.

On merely playing over some of Pedrell's music, three striking qualities are immediately perceptible. There are individual peculiarities in his style, serenity as well as strength in his emotions, and an unusual sense of mystery, or of poetry — a sense which Falla calls the " power of evocation (*poder evocativo*)." A more detailed examination reveals the fact that these qualities are derived — apart from his own natural gifts — from his assimilation of traditional melodies and his study of the music of primitive times.

Pedrell himself has related in the introduction to his *Cancionero* how, almost from infancy, he tried to write down songs, street cries, and all sorts of music he heard, from the lullaby with which his

6

mother put his younger brother to sleep in the cradle to the marches played by military bands in the street. This exercise, laboriously undertaken at the suggestion of the master who taught him his notes, came to be the most attractive game of his childhood. Then, as a choir-boy in the cathedral of his native place, Tortosa, he had splendid opportunities for making practical acquaintance with many kinds of church-music, as well as being filled with awe at those mysterious, primitive chants (with words in the vernacular) which were still in use in some Spanish cathedrals. There was one in particular, "*In recort* . . . In memory . . . (of the Passion), preserved by Pedrell in his *Cancionero,* which, he used to declare, had terrified him, whenever he heard it.

At the time that the score of his opera *Los Pirineos* was printed, in 1894, Pedrell published a pamphlet, *Por nuestra música (For the sake of our music)* in which he sought to explain his principles. This pamphlet in a French translation was widely read in Europe, particularly in Germany, and prepared the way for the European reputation which Pedrell was afterwards to win, through his editions of Victoria and of the Spanish composers of the " golden century," his excellent catalogue of the music in the Biblioteca Catalana at Barcelona, and his learned articles in the *Sammelbände der Internationalen Musikgesellschaft.*

Pedrell's point of departure was a saying of

7

Padre Eximeno,[2] that folk-song was the basis upon which the cultivated music of every people should be constructed. To this Pedrell added:

" The character of any music which is truly national is to be met with not only in folk-song and in the instinctive music of primitive epochs, but also in works of genius and in the masterpieces of the great periods of the art."

He goes on to name the conditions necessary to the existence of a national art of music: " an unbroken tradition, characteristics which are of general occurrence and permanent duration, essential agreement between different examples of the art, and the use of determinate native forms which some unconscious power has made adequate to the genius of the race, to its customs and temperament."

Falla's comments on the program set forth by Pedrell are very interesting, for they show us the mind of the pupil as well as of the master. Pedrell (he says), in spite of his constant familiarity with the Spanish classics and the fervent devotion he felt for them, had the necessary conviction and strength of mind not to be led astray by musical devices which were mere conventions. His treatment never passed beyond the limits of the music. " And yet," he adds,

[2] An acute and learned Jesuit of the eighteenth century, who, on the expulsion of his order from Spain, and of himself from the chair of mathematics in the military academy at Segovia, repaired to Rome and devoted his talents (which were considerable) to the study of music.

" what wealth is hidden under this apparent modesty! And how arduous and profound the labour of extracting the harmonic mysteries contained in a traditional melody! "

Pedrell made a renaissance possible in Spanish music because he excavated the facts of Spanish musical tradition both cultivated and popular. " He loved his art," Falla adds, " with a vehemence which I have rarely seen equalled, and he preserved his vigorous faith and his noble enthusiasm until the end of his life." Two months before his death, at the age of eighty-one, he wrote on the occasion of the congress of *cante hondo* (primitive Andalucian folksong) organized by Falla at Granada in 1922: " Tell your friends that I am singing *cante hondo* inside me; if I am not with you in the flesh, I am and ever shall be with you in spirit, with all my soul."

Andalucian *cante hondo* was, as Pedrell knew well, by no means the only form of Spanish folksong. His *Cancionero* is a magnificent treasury of native music. Spanish folk-music, unlike the greater part of our own folk-music in England, has needed no rediscovery. In most parts of Spain it is still alive and still growing; the music-hall *cuplé* has affected, but has not yet killed it. Spanish folk-music, however, is notable for its local differences; and the size of the country, its mountainous nature, and the difficulty of communications have made the differences far more pronounced. Tunes from Galicia in the

north-west, from the Basque Provinces under the
northern end of the Pyrenees, from Catalonia on
the Mediterranean coast, and from Andalucía in the
south-west, are as different as tunes can possibly be.
Yet there is one accidental point of likeness between
folk-song in Spain and in Great Britain. The kind of
Spanish music, cultivated or popular, which is best
known outside the Peninsula, the only kind which
many people and many musicians immediately recognize as Spanish, is the kind which comes from Andalucía; while foreign musicians are generally convinced that the only folk-music in the British Isles is
that which belongs to the "Celtic fringe." The
"England" of the Spanish peninsula is Castile; and
Castilian folk-music, like English folk-music, has
lately been coming into its own. The songs from the
eastern counties collected by Vaughan Williams (and
his settings of them, which brought out the inmost
essence of the melodies in a way which had not been
achieved since the days of Purcell or the Elizabethans), the Somerset songs collected by Cecil
Sharp, and, not least, the old English melodies collected by him in the Appalachian Mountains of
Virginia have a parallel in Spain in the songs from
Burgos collected by Olmeda, from Salamanca by
Ledesma, and from the Asturias by E. M. Torner,
selected and arranged with many others in the *Cancionero* of Pedrell. Again, as there are folk-songs in
England which can be traced back to the time of

Purcell or the Elizabethans, so some Castilian tunes may be traced back to those quoted by Salinas, who was professor of music at Salamanca in the time of Philip II. The discovery of tunes to some of the old Border ballads in Northumberland may be compared with the finding of both words and music of the old Spanish *romances* still being sung, by washerwomen, and many other country people on many other occasions, in remote parts of Castile and the Asturias; and it is fortunate that the greatest living authority on Spanish ballads, Don Ramón Menéndez Pidal, is musician enough to realize the interest and importance of the melodies to which the ballads are sung.

Pedrell's *Cancionero* is the best possible introduction to this great body of traditional Spanish music;[3] and his accompaniments, to which some musicians of today might take exception, generally succeed in their object and provide a background for the tune thoroughly in keeping with its modal, rhythmical, and other musical characteristics. Pedrell never used a folk-tune as an excuse for a display of virtuosity on his own account; his unassuming accompaniments have the appearance of being written for use in the lecture-room and are seldom suitable for the more brilliant requirements of the concert-hall. A Northern musician to whom I showed the book put it down with no more than the remark that he

[3] It was published through the disinterested efforts of Don Juan Gisbert, though his name appears in no part of any of the four volumes.

didn't like the accompaniments. In the same way, a musical critic in Madrid dismissed a good orchestral arrangement of the "Londonderry Air" as merely clever, and never noticed the tune at all; while a Spanish acquaintance dismissed the exquisite singing of south Italian folk-songs by Geni Sadero as "*una lata*" because the pianoforte accompaniments were (as they certainly are) somewhat inadequate and distracting.

Falla's feelings in regard to Pedrell's *Cancionero* are best given in his own words: "The *Cancionero*," he says, "is like some precious casket, which has preserved the essential music of our inmost thoughts and feelings and can thrill us with its magical power of evoking times and places made famous in the history and legend of the Spanish peninsula."

Yet (he goes on) if it contains such wealth for all in whom the power of feeling is still alive, what teaching does it promise to the Spanish musician?

In those pages he will find, not only a varied and abundant display of our natural music, but also the many different effects, both modal and harmonic, produced from the rhythmical and melodic substance of that music.

The simple comparison of some of the melodies taken down and harmonized by Pedrell, with the transcription and harmonization of the same melodies in collections which preceded his, will prove how a song which we hardly noticed when we read it in the older collections has acquired a rare value and significance when presented in Pedrell's *Cancionero.*

The fact is that the modal and highly individual character of certain Spanish melodies has been transcribed by some collectors with the invariable tonal feeling of the major and minor scales; while Pedrell extracted from these melodies their true essence, both modal and harmonic. Yet the Cancionero can offer even more than this. It can show us the process of evolution at work in popular melodies, and the treatment of them by Spanish musicians in both primitive and classical times, from the thirteenth century to the seventeenth.

This is not the place for a detailed study of Pedrell's compositions. My intention has been to demonstrate — as far as possible in the words of Falla, his best pupil — how great is the significance of Pedrell in contemporary Spanish music; and to do so is the more important in that certain writers on the subject have been inclined to grudge Pedrell the credit that was due to him. Not even Falla would proclaim that either the works or the ideas of the master are beyond criticism. There are points upon which doubts are permissible and others upon which judgment must be reserved; moreover the significance which can be legitimately attributed to his later works cannot be maintained for those which preceded *Los Pirineos.*

Since Pedrell, and even — in some quarters —

Falla himself, have been dismissed as "mere 'folk-lore' composers," it is well to have Falla's own opinion on the subject, expressed as nearly as possible in his own words: "The inclusion of fragments of music from the Spanish classics which Pedrell permitted in some of his works, and also his frequent employment of folk-songs in their traditional forms, may be somewhat questionable proceedings; but they in no way strike at the root of the doctrine already proclaimed by the Master, and should indeed be considered as special, if somewhat wide, applications of that doctrine."

Contrary to what is generally believed, in Falla's works there are practically no quotations, and the one instance in which he has made use of Spanish folk-songs in their traditional form is the collection of *Seven Spanish Songs*, in which characteristic folk-songs of the Peninsula have been provided with pianoforte accompaniments which are at the same time brilliantly pianistic and yet thoroughly in keeping with the spirit of the original melodies.

Falla's music, however, with the exception of *The Puppet-Show* and the Harpsichord Concerto, is in a style that is recognizable everywhere as "the Spanish idiom." An attempt must be made to discover what this means.

CHAPTER II

THE SPANISH IDIOM

In spite of all the Spanish music which has been heard in recent years, the only kind which many people — even Spanish people — can immediately recognize as "Spanish" remains substantially what it was fifty years ago; while modern Spanish music which does not conform to this type is apt to be coldly received and never played again. The type was definitely established in Europe by the production of *Carmen* in 1876, and then spread by such works as Lalo's *Capriccio* and the pianoforte duets of Moszkowski, while it was treated by Chabrier as a splendid joke. Yet it had existed before, particularly in the comic operas (*zarzuelas*) of Barbieri (1823–94), and in one or two later Spanish comic operas in the same style which somehow went round the world.

The origins of this "Spanish style" are very interesting. There often seems to be a suggestion of street-music about it (as there is in much of the instrumental music of Schubert), and traces of the style can be found as far back as the seventeenth century. It may be detected in the old Spanish theatre-music first published by Pedrell, and in the popular

15

— not to say vulgar — church-music of the time: *villancicos* sung to Spanish words, most of which still remains in the decent obscurity of the National Library at Madrid. It is possible to trace the style even further back: to the little pieces sung by shepherds in the dramatic entertainments of Juan del Enzina, whose musical compositions date from between 1483 and 1494.

Yet, whatever its remoter origins, the " Spanish style " is largely a creation of the eighteenth century. It is found unmistakably in the popular — or popularized — musical performances known as *tonadillas,* which arose as a national reaction to the dictatorship of Italian singers and the Italian opera and could only be performed by singers who had been born and bred in Spain and more particularly in Andalucía. Such were " La Tirana," immortalized in the portrait by Goya, and " La Caramba," who has achieved a different kind of immortality owing to the fact that her stage-name (derived from a striking form of beribboned head-dress) has become a familiar euphemism with all Spanish-speaking peoples to express considerable surprise. Another famous singer of *tonadillas* was Manuel García, the founder of the celebrated family of great singers, who (as we shall see) was probably the first to convey " the Spanish style " to the rest of Europe.

Descriptions of social functions in which such street-music had a place are to be found in the travel-diaries of William Beckford, particularly among the entries relating to his stay in Madrid in 1787. As a cultivated man of the world, Beckford naturally accepted and supported the Italian opera and delighted in the performances of Italian singers. But he had also a certain interest, and a certain power of discrimination, in music which was definitely Spanish and which he, as an intelligent traveller, thought it his duty to hear while he was in Spain. And while he could find little but expressions of the most stately invective for the " untoward minstrels " who played upon " humstrums and hurdy-gurdies or the devil knows best what kind of instruments" in the street, and prevented him from sleeping, he could still long for " the rapturous *Seguidillas* of which I have heard such wonders." He scandalized a great gathering at which the Duchess of Osuna was present, with Boccherini as conductor of her private band, by appearing in the dress of a *majo* (familiar from the paintings and tapestries of Goya) and insisting on the performance of *boleros* and other street-music of the time.

It is, curiously enough, from the street-music of that time that the Spanish effects in *Carmen* are mainly derived.

Carmen has become, for the non-Spanish world, the mirror of the Spanish soul, the pattern of Spanish music. Yet Carmen herself is by no means a normal Spanish type, or even an abnormal Spanish type which is specifically Spanish, and the few genuinely

Spanish touches in the music are not derived directly from folk-song. The *habanera,* sung by Carmen on her first entry, was imitated from a Spanish song, but it was a song written by the Spanish-American composer Yradier, who died in 1865. "Yradier certainly does not deserve to be ranked among the masters; yet this musician of Spanish America had so absorbed the impressions of his environment that he could seize and record intonations and rhythms sufficiently different from those of European music to afford a superficial satisfaction to amateurs of exotic sensations. He was [an] intermediary between the anonymous authors of folk-songs and the veritable creators of art." [1]

It was from another such intermediary, the great Manuel García, that the other definitely Spanish moment in *Carmen* is derived: the orchestral interlude played before the last act of the opera. Bizet found it in a collection of Spanish songs known as *Echos d'Espagne* and published in Paris in 1872, while the editor of this collection took it from a *polo* (a wild Andalucian song) in *El Criado fingido,* a *tonadilla* written by Manuel García and first sung by him in Madrid in 1804.[2] How far this was an original composition of the great singer is open to question. The

[1] Julien Tiersot: "Bizet and Spanish Music" (*Musical Quarterly,* October 1927. Also in *Le Ménestrel,* 1925).

[2] The *polo* has been reprinted by Mitjana in the volume referring to Spain in the *Encyclopédie de la Musique et Dictionnaire du Conservatoire,* pp. 2296–9.

polo is one of the older forms of Andalucian folk-
song, and the *polo* in *El Criado fingido* seems to have
certain traditional features, in both the melody and
the accompaniment, though here both melody and
accompaniment have been conventionalized in the
manner of popular singers — and street singers — of
eighteenth-century Madrid. Bizet touched it with his
genius, without destroying its popular, eighteenth-
century Spanish character; but in the rest of the
opera Bizet's genius is so great and his music so original that (as Mr. Pedro Morales has remarked)
"Everybody thought, after the first and long expected success, that it was pure Spanish, and this be-
lief still remains. But the fact is, that of the immense
variety of popular melodies to be found in Spain, the
great composer, faithful to the intended local colour
of the libretto, only used (besides the rhythm of the
habanera) two or three Andalucian tunes, which in
his hands forcibly become French as the development
goes on."

Yet the *polo,* however conventionalized it may be
in *Carmen* or in the *tonadilla* of Manuel García, is
really a traditional form of southern Spanish folk-
song — one of those primitive Andalucian melodies
which are known by the name of *cante hondo.*

As I have tried on more than one occasion [3] to
explain what *cante hondo* is, and the relation it bears

[3] *The Music of Spanish History* (Hispanic Society of America
and Oxford University Press, 1926). *Spain from the South* (London
and New York, 1928).

to *cante flamenco,* I may perhaps be forgiven if, in a book concerned with Falla and Spanish music, I endeavour to do so as nearly as possible in Falla's own words, relying principally on the pamphlet on the subject which he published at the time of the first festival of *cante hondo,* held at Granada in 1922.[4]

In the history of Spain (he begins) there are three events which, though varying in their effect on general life and culture, have been of considerable importance in the history of music. They are:

(1) the adoption by the Spanish Church of Byzantine liturgical music;

(2) the Muslim invasion; and

(3) the immigration and establishment in Spain of numerous bands of gipsies.

Pedrell, in his *Cancionero,* was of opinion that the persistence of oriental characteristics in various Spanish folk-songs was due to Byzantine influence, which appeared in the chants used in the Spanish Church from the time of the conversion of the country to Christianity down to the eleventh century, when the Roman liturgy, so-called, was introduced in its place.

[4] *El "Cante Jondo" (Canto primitivo andaluz)* (Granada, Editorial Urania, 1922). Lengthy extracts were afterwards published in the *Revue musicale,* but the original Spanish has been used in the pages which follow.

"*Hondo*" (or, in its provincial, strongly aspirated form "*jondo*") signifies "deep" "profound"; the song of the depths, of the tragic sense of life, of prisons and *prostíbolos.*

To this Falla would add that in one of the Andalucian types of melody, and one of the most primitive — the *siguiriya* — certain elements of Byzantine chant are still to be found. There are the modes of the primitive systems (which should not be confused with the modes now called Greek, although the latter sometimes partake of the structure of the former); the enharmonism inherent in the primitive modes (that is to say, the division and subdivision of the indeterminate passing-notes — *notas sensibles* — in their functions as determining the genus); and, lastly, the absence of metrical rhythm in the melodic line and its wealth of modulating inflexions.

Such characteristics are also to be found, at times, in Moorish songs of Andalucian origin — which are (of course) of a later date than that of the adoption of Byzantine music by the Spanish Church; and this led Pedrell to affirm that " Spanish music owes nothing essential to the Arabs or the Moors, who probably did no more than reform certain ornamental figures common to the oriental and Persian systems, from which Arab music was derived. It follows that those who were influenced were [not the Spaniards, but] the Moors."

We must suppose (Falla continues) that Pedrell, in making this statement, was referring to the purely melodic music of the Moors of Andalucía; for it cannot be doubted that in other forms of this music, and especially in dance-music, there are elements, both rhythmical and melodic, which will be looked for in vain in Spanish liturgical music. It is an undoubted fact not only that the kind of music still known in Morocco, Algiers, and Tunis as "Andaluz music of the Moors of Granada" has preserved peculiar features which distinguish it from music of Arabic origin, but also that in its rhythmical dance forms a Spanish musician can easily recognize the origin of many Andalucian forms: *sevillanos, zapateados, seguidillas,* etc.

Yet beyond the Byzantine element and the Arab element, there are in the melody of the *siguiriya* peculiarities which are, it seems, independent features, unaffected by primitive Christian chants and Moorish music from Granada. Where have these peculiarities come from? In Falla's opinion, they come from the gipsy tribes which established themselves in Spain in the fifteenth century. These tribes, coming from the East, gave Andalucian folk-song, *cante andaluz,* that new musical character which constitutes *cante hondo.* It is the resultant of the forces mentioned above and not exclusively an effect due to any of the peoples which have worked together to produce them. The primeval, Andalucian nature has fused them and formed a new kind of music with the accretions which it has received elsewhere.

What has been just said will be made clearer if we analyse the musical features which distinguish *cante hondo.* This name is given to a group of Andalucian folk-songs, the type of which Falla believes to be the so-called *siguiriya gitana* (*gipsy seguidilla*) from which are derived other types of melody — for example, *polos, martinetes,* and *soleares* [5] — which still exist and which preserve certain characteristics of the highest musical interest, distinguishing them from the more modern groups formed by the songs commonly called *flamenco.* [6] Strictly speaking, however, that name should only be applied to the more modern group, comprising *malagueñas, granadinas, rondeñas* (from which the first two are derived), *sevillanas, peteneras,* [7] and others, which are also derivations from those already mentioned.

In *cante hondo* Falla finds analogies with certain types of melody found in India and elsewhere in the East. The positions of the smaller intervals in the scale are not invariable; their production depends upon the raising or lowering of the voice due to the expression given to the word which is being sung. This leads to the free alteration of four of the seven tones of the scale; that is to say, only three are fixed; while, further, each of the notes susceptible of

[5] The derivation of the first two of these is difficult and uncertain. "*Soleares*" is the plural of "*soleá,*" a provincial or gipsy form of "*soledad* (solitude)."

[6] For the somewhat problematical origins of this word see Grove's *Dictionary,* third edition, or *Spain from the South,* Chapter I.

[7] The first four of these names are geographical, signifying songs from Málaga, Granada, Ronda, and Seville, while " La Petenera " is said to have been a singer of these songs in the middle of the last century. See also S. de Madariaga, *Shelley and Calderon, and other Essays* (1920).

alteration is divided and subdivided, resulting in certain cases in the alteration of the notes of attack and resolution of some fragments of the phrase. To this may be added the *portamento* of the voice — that manner of singing which produces the infinite gradations of pitch existing between two notes, whether next to each other or far apart.[8]

Another peculiarity of *cante hondo* is the employment of a compass which rarely exceeds the limits of a sixth. "This sixth, of course, is not composed solely of nine semitones as is the case with our tempered scale. By the employment of the enharmonic genus, there is a considerable increase in the number of tones which the singer can produce."

Thirdly, *cante hondo* provides examples of the repetition of the same note — to the point of obsession — frequently accompanied by an appoggiatura from above or below. "This proceeding is characteristic of certain formulas of enchantment, and even of certain chants used for recitation. . . . By its means certain melodies of the group under consideration achieve the destruction of all metrical feeling

[8] " Summing up what has been said, we may affirm, firstly, that in *cante hondo* (as equally in the primitive melodies of the East) the musical scale is the direct consequence of what might be called the oral scale. . . . What we have called ' modulation by enharmonism ' may be considered as more or less a consequence of the primitive enharmonic genus. This consequence is, however, more apparent than real, seeing that our tempered scale only permits us to change the functions of one note; while in enharmonism, properly so-called, that tone is modified according to the natural necessities of its functions as determining the genus " (Falla).

and give the impression that it is a piece of prose which is being sung, when in reality the text is in verse."

Although gipsy melody is rich in ornamental figures, these (as in primitive oriental music) are only exployed at determinate moments as lyrical expansion or as passionate outbursts suggested by the strong emotions described in the text. "They may be considered, therefore, as extended vocal inflexions rather than as ornamental figures, although they assume the form of the latter on being translated into the geometrical intervals of the tempered scale."

Lastly, *cante hondo* is remarkable for the cries of *" Olé, olé! "* [9] with which the audience encourages the *cantaores* and *tocaores,* the singers and players; and this, too, is a custom still observed in analogous cases by races of oriental origin.

It should not be thought (Falla continues) that the *siguiriya* and its derivatives are simply melodies transplanted from the East to the West. "We are dealing at the most with a graft — or, better, with a coincidence of origins — which has assuredly not been revealed in a single, determinate moment, but has followed from the accumulated historical facts which have for long been developing in the Peninsula. And this is the reason why the melodies peculiar to Andalucía, though they coincide in their essential elements with those of peoples widely separated

[9] Sometimes interpreted as an invocation to Allah: *" Yallah! "*

25

geographically from Spain, yet show an intimate character which is so individual and so national as to make them quite unmistakable."

It is important to make clear what the characteristics of *cante hondo* really are, since it is not only threatened with ruin, but is on the point of disappearing for ever. The glowing descriptions of musical performances in southern Spain given in such numbers by writers who are not musicians, and the romantic religiosity attributed by certain professors to the singing of *saetas* in Seville during the processions of Holy Week, apply not to the true *cante hondo,* but to a vulgarized form of it which has received the name of *cante flamenco.*[10] The truth seems to be that except for some few *cantaores* and one or two who have grown too old to sing, that which remains of the primitive Andaluz folk-song is only the shadow of what it once was.

" The grave, hieratic melody of yesterday has degenerated into the ridiculous *flamenco* style of today, in which those elements which once con-

[10] I was in Seville once with Falla during Holy Week. We had wandered one evening into some remote quarter to see the procession bring back the statue of the saint to the parish church. The procession stopped, and a rasping voice began a *saeta* in a style which even a foreigner could recognize for a complete travesty of the real thing. Falla was furious. " They call that singing *saetas?* " he cried. " It sounds like drawing corks — like someone going to be sick! " " Hush, man," they said, " for God's sake! Rabbits, man! . . ." and became so threatening that I contrived to draw him away to another part of the crowd.

stituted its glory and its ancient title of nobility have been adulterated and modernized. The sober modulations of the voice — the natural inflexions of the melody which provoke the division and subdivision of the tones of the scale — have been converted into a succession of artificial, ornamental figures, more suitable to the decadent practice of the worst period of Italian opera than to the primitive melodies of the orient. . . . The limits of the reduced melodic compass in which the melodies were evolved have been stupidly increased, and for the modal wealth of the ancient scales has been substituted the tonal poverty caused by the general use of the major and minor scales. . . . And, lastly, the phrase, clumsily reduced to metre, is daily losing that rhythmic flexibility which constituted one of its greatest beauties."

These are words which the ecstatic traveller and the cynical director of personally conducted tours might take to heart. The alert musician will remember that something of the same kind has been taking place in other countries, and more particularly in Hungary.

The cases of Spain and Hungary offer curious analogies. The recent musical revivals have taken place at the same time as the rediscovery of the genuine folk-songs of the country, as distinguished from the familiar songs which had formerly passed as such; and these folk-song movements, if not altogether the cause of the revivals, have yet had a decided influence upon them. In Hungary the experiences of folk-song collectors have been much the same as in England and Spain. The type of Hungarian music known to Europe through the rhapsodies and dances of Liszt and Brahms proved on investigation to have arisen mainly at the beginning of the nineteenth century. Béla Bartók, Zoltan Kodály, and others discovered that there was a much older kind of peasant music, both in Hungary as it now is and in those parts of the old kingdom which have lately been annexed to other countries. Several thousand melodies were collected — chiefly by phonographic recording, a method which has unfortunately been but little used in Spain — and for comparison Bartók made an excursion to Biskra, where he investigated and recovered Arab music as it was actually performed. The oldest kind of music in Hungary, he found, was represented by melodies in a vague, free, declamatory style; but there were also many others of more recent origin, which had a characteristic "snap" in the rhythm: something — though not exactly — like that of an English newspaper boy, when he shouts: "Ex — tra special," or like that in the tune in *The Beggar's Opera* which begins: "Cease your funning, Force and cunning. . . ."

Bartók seems somewhat sceptical on the question of oriental (Turkish) influence on Hungarian music. In Spain, on the contrary, it is usual for writers (and

particularly non-Spanish writers) to attribute to
"Moorish influence" anything which they do not
immediately apprehend, in music and everything else;
so that any feature which is not easy to explain is
labelled "oriental" to avoid further inquiry, while
characteristics which may really be of oriental origin
are neglected or attributed to some other cause. Muslim influence is certainly more probable in Spain than
in Hungary. There were Muslims in Spain, it will be
remembered, for nearly nine hundred years: from
the invasion of 711 until the final expulsion of the
Moriscos at the beginning of the seventeenth century; while the Turkish occupation of Hungary only
began after the battle of Mohács in 1526 and ended
not long after the seige of Vienna in 1683. In neither
Hungary nor Spain was the subjugation complete;
north-west Hungary remained Christian, Transylva-
nia owed only a nominal allegiance to the Turks, and
the pashas of Pest never ruled over a cultivated,
musical society like the caliphs of Córdoba. Most important of all, the singers of folk-songs in Hungary
(the peasants) were the slaves, while the Muslims
were the masters; but in Spain the proportion of
Muslims among the peasants was always high, and in
the times of the caliphate of Córdoba the Christians
lived principally in the towns. It has been shown
that Turkish influence on the music of another race
(for example, on the church-music of the Arme-
nians, has led to an extravagant use of decoration; the

original rhythms and melodies were buried under an elaborate embroidery of runs, turns, trills, and grace-notes. In Spain this tendency to profuse ornamentation is seen in every form of art, whether cultivated or popular, deliberate or spontaneous, and it is a tendency which undoubtedly goes back to the time of the Moors.

Again, the rhythm of the accompanying instrument seems less sophisticated in Hungary than in most parts of Spain. It is conceived on a different principle and in its simplest form is represented by the drone of the bagpipes, blowing a single note throughout the performance. To Muslims, on the contrary, anything approaching harmony was abhorrent, illogical, and enervating (at least in theory) — and the drone is harmony reduced to its lowest terms. Rhythm and combinations of conflicting rhythms produced by instruments of percussion were, and are still, the only kind of accompaniment permitted in Muslim music. The irresistible rhythms of Hungarian dances have often been described and have bewitched all who have ever felt them. Yet rhythm in Hungary is far simpler than it is in Spain; for in Spain a single good player on the castanets, for instance, can produce a combination of rhythms (and even a subtle contrast of tone-colour) which in its emotional effect is unsurpassed in the whole range of Spanish music.

Falla in Spain, like Bartók in Hungary, has worked hard to disinter the older forms of melody as they were before the vulgarization which set in at the beginning of the last century. It was to that end that he organized the competitive festival of *cante hondo* which was held at Granada in 1922.[11] The cause of the change in the music of both countries may have been the same. It was the popularity of gipsy musicians, and the imitation of gipsy ways of playing and singing by performers who were not gipsies; and it led to what one would like to call the "gipsification" of the older melodies. This curious phase of social history, this sudden popularity of gipsy musicians and the aping of their manner of performances may have been due to the romantic movement, or to the unsettled state of society which was the legacy of the Napoleonic wars — for, needless to say, there had been gipsy musicians for centuries, in both Spain and Hungary. In Spain the transition was taking place about the time of Borrow and Ford, Gautier and Mérimée; and the atmosphere is faithfully represented in the original story of *Carmen*, before it was travestied by the opera librettists to make it agree with "romantic Spain" as that country of the imagination was understood in Paris.

It is impossible to leave the subject of the "Spanish idiom" without some reference to the accompanying instrument — the Spanish guitar. Falla expresses its function in this way: The guitar (he says) as popularly used in Spain represents two distinct musical

---

[11] *The Music of Spanish History*, pp. 1-4.

effects: that of the rhythm, which is apparent and immediately perceptible, and that of the harmony. The
former, in conjunction with certain forms of cadence,
has been for long the only effect employed in more or
less cultivated music, while the importance of the
latter—the effect which is tonal, harmonic—has
hardly been recognized by composers, except Domenico Scarlatti, until recent times. The Russians seem
to have been the first to be aware of it, but, with the
exception of Glinka, none of them knew of it except
by hearsay, or imagined that the peculiar manner of
playing of the people of Andalucía could be applied
to artistic music. Even Glinka paid more attention to
ornament and cadence than to the inner, harmonic
phenomena produced by this method of playing. Debussy, however, managed, to a certain extent, to in-
corporate these effects into his music; his harmonic
texture gives proof of it in several instances. His example led to brilliant consequences: the *Iberia* of
Isaac Albéniz.

The man who made modern Spanish music
known to the rest of Europe was Enrique Granados.
Albéniz, an older man, had written more for the
pianoforte and had composed and produced operas
to libretti by an Englishman — the late Lord Laty-
mer. But Granados seemed to bring something that
was new into pianoforte music, and his fame was
definitely established when it became known that he
had gone down in the *Sussex*, torpedoed in the Eng-

lish Channel in 1916. What Granados introduced into the music of northern Europe might be described as a gesture. " Stately Spanish grace " is the first thing that strikes one in such a piece as " *Los Requiebros* " in the first book of the *Goyescas*. In his way of writing for the pianoforte he owed much to Liszt; the texture of his music is definitely nineteenth-century — that is to say, German. Yet his sense of form — or, as some critics hastily conclude, the absence of it — was also new; he rambled on, making his points by repetition (like a Spanish poet) and saying the same thing in a number of delightful and decorative ways. Granados, with his alert Catalan intelligence, was quick to seize upon the effective qualities of the music of other times and other regions. He rearranged (though it was a pity to tamper with them) some of the harpsichord sonatas of Domenico Scarlatti, who through his long residence in Spain is regarded as the founder of Spanish pianoforte style; and he composed several books of *tonadillas*, in the manner of eighteenth-century Spanish songs. His masterpiece is the famous collection of *Goyescas* — pianoforte pieces (which were afterwards rather unfortunately worked up into an opera) suggested by scenes from the paintings of Goya.

Albéniz was also a Catalan by birth; and though he sometimes made use of tunes from his own country, he preferred as a rule to draw upon Andalucía. His last works, the four books of pianoforte pieces known as *Iberia,* are brilliant studies of characteristic rhythms and effects from different parts of Spain, often developed with a great sense of poetical suggestion. They are very much in " the Spanish idiom "; but it is the Spanish idiom employed by a master, and in the best of them — for example, " *Evocación* " (which contrasts a tune in the style of Navarre with a tune in the style of Andalucía), " *El Albaicín,*" " *El Puerto,*" " *Almería* " — one can forget the " *idiom* " in the beauty of the musical thought; while even " Triana," if it contains nothing much besides the " *idiom,*" always surprises and pleases with its ingenuities of colour, its suggestions of the tambourine, and the snatches of *cante hondo* from across the river. The more one gets to know these pieces of Albéniz, the more it becomes apparent that " the Spanish idiom " is something to which one has to become so accustomed that one no longer notices it — in other words, it is impossible to see what a composer means until his idiom is so familiar that one is no longer distracted by it.

There is, as has been already stated, much Spanish music, and much musical material in Spain, which shows no trace of the Spanish idiom as it is usually recognized. Considerable use has been made of this in Catalonia, Guridi has drawn largely on Basque tunes, while Granados (for example, in " *La Maja y el ruiseñor* " in the *Goyescas*) achieved a wonderful evocation of the music of Castile. Regional music in

34

Spain has, of course, been made an instrument of separatist propaganda. It is the privilege of a musician, and the obligation of an English or American musician, to preserve a strict neutrality and make as many friends as he can.

CHAPTER III

FALLA IN "ARABIA"

The corner of Spain to which Falla belongs — the province of Andalucía and the former kingdom of Granada — is different from other parts of Europe and from other parts of Spain. It could only be described adequately by saying that it is like Mr. Walter de la Mare's "Arabia" come true; and a reader of English poetry who wishes to get the full flavour of Falla's music should begin by saying that exquisite poem over to himself. To know the music of "Arabia," he must " descry her gliding streams," he must

> Hear her strange lutes on the green banks
> Ring loud with the grief and delight
> Of the dim-silked, dark-haired musicians
> In the brooding silence of night.

That is the background against which music — Falla, Albéniz, Debussy, and Domenico Scarlatti — is performed. It is played in gardens on summer nights on a trio of "twangling" instruments; and such a performance is, for a musician, the supreme and unsurpassable moment of a visit to Spain. No music will ever sound quite the same again.

It was soon after my first meeting with Falla, in 1919, that I was able to experience this; and the memory of it has remained with me as one of the most vivid and most beautiful that I can ever hope to have. It would take too long to describe that evening again,[1] or to relate how at the end of it, when we had all gone up into a tower for the sake of the view, we shouted with one voice for the music of Falla, and in the darkness beneath us the dim musicians played until they could play no more. The performance consisted of a trio of a guitar and two Spanish mandolins (*laúd* and *bandurria*) playing arrangements of pianoforte pieces by Albéniz, Barrios, Debussy, and Falla. The musicians had taken their "strange lutes" to a place in the garden which had been carefully chosen before they arrived. It was below the terrace so that they might be hidden from view, and close to a pool so that the utmost resonance might be obtained from the water. The trio of bright, clear-sounding instruments seemed something new in musical sound. They were played so that the intimate structure of the music — its "works," so to speak — were clearly and unmistakably revealed and the beauty (or, it might be, the inadequacy) of the workmanship more easy to recognize. It was as if the music were being held up to the light to see how beautiful

[1] See *A Picture of Modern Spain* (London, 1921), pp. 237–45.

it was, or being X-rayed to see what was the matter with it. In the strange delight of that starlit garden it could be realized how perfectly the sparkling clearness of the plucked instruments was suited to the open air. Yet it was by no means a case of romantic *Nachtmusik*. There was nothing hidden or mysterious about it. Above all and over all was the clear, tranquil night, with the serene and marvellous radiance of the stars. One could think clearly, more clearly than usual, and listen to music more easily than ever before — or since.

I was able to make closer acquaintance with the guitar in a house just outside the Alhambra. The player, whose father's house it was, Don Angel Barrios, is a composer of distinction and one of the best guitarists in Spain. On hot summer nights Falla and he would sit on the *patio*, where by means of a towel the fountain had been muffled, but not altogether silenced, and the guitar would be ingeniously transposed into a sharp key by the *cejuela* (or *capotasto*), screwed across the end of the finger-board. As autumn came on, we took refuge in a small room hung with hams and sausages and lined with little kegs of *manzanilla*; and when Falla was confined to his bedroom with a cold, Barrios would come every evening with his guitar. I learnt then that the guitar, as he played it, was not merely a part of the "national legend," or "one of the signs of national barbarity," as some Spaniards declare, but a thoroughly serious

38

and admirable instrument. Falla has always treated the guitar seriously; and when the editor of the *Revue musicale* invited him to send something "*pour le tombeau de Claude Debussy*," he wrote his *Homenaje* for the guitar, and it was first tried over in his room at one of the meetings I have described.

Falla believes intensely in the future of the guitar. . . . But at this point some reader may interrupt with a certain show of contempt: "Future? I should have thought it an instrument of the past: one *with* a past, at all events!" It is true that, with us, the idea of "playing on the Spanish guitar" has somehow acquired a curiously disreputable significance, while the instrument itself is — or was until the arrival of Andrés Segovia — regarded as a piece of romantic stage furniture. "No," says Falla. "Not at all! Romantic times were precisely those in which the guitar was at its worst; and then, of course, it spread all over Europe. It was made to play the sort of music that other instruments played, but it was not really suitable for nineteenth-century music, and so it dropped out. It is coming back again, because it is peculiarly adapted for modern music."

He went on to explain why. The six strings of the guitar are tuned in fourths, with a third in the middle: E, A, D, G, B, E. That instruments tuned in fifths are not particularly apt for modern music might be suspected from the fact that the technique of the violin has practically stood still since the days

39

of Paganini. By means of daring *scordature* Paganini was able to do what very few modern violinists would care to attempt now, for the violin is a "high-tension" instrument as it is, and the general tendency of modern orchestras is towards a further rise of pitch for the sake of brilliance. Moreover, in spite of the studies by Sor, and the beautifully executed transcriptions with which Segovia has made us familiar, music of the later eighteenth and nineteenth centuries does not seem so apt for the guitar as music written since the time of Debussy. This is due partly to Debussy's harmonic scheme and to his widening of the range of harmonic and rhythmic expression (which came to him from the study of Spanish and oriental music), and partly also to the clearness of the texture of his music, which was necessary to bring out all its subtleties of rhythm and colour. It is partly due also to the fact that modern composers have grown tired of the smoothness and fullness of massed strings supported by a rich round tone in the brass and are aiming at something clearer, in which bowed instruments have a comparatively small part.

Paganini also wrote for the guitar; but it is interesting to observe his elementary treatment of that instrument (a strange contrast to his treatment of the violin) as shown in the quartets for guitar and strings, written for drawing-room use and "*dedicati alle amatrici.*"

The guitar in Spain is not a drawing-room instrument; indeed, the circumstances under which it is often used are as remote from a drawing-room as anything in Europe, and in the hands of quite an ordinary player it can be made to do astonishing things. The effects of harmony produced unconsciously by guitarists in Andalucía are among the marvels of untutored art. There are two methods of playing. *Rasguear,* "thrumming," consists of repeated chords in which all the five or six notes are seldom changed at once, and the notes which are held on — to steady the hand — produce an "internal pedal-point" such as we find in the sonatas of Domenico Scarlatti. *Puntear,* on the other hand, is the playing of different notes in succession. It is probable (Falla says) that the Spanish instrumentalists of the sixteenth century were among the first to play an accompaniment of repeated chords to a vocal or instrumental melody. Further, from the earliest times a distinction has been made in Spain between the *guitarra latina* (playing chords) and the *guitarra morisca* (playing melodies) ; while to this day the popular *gembri* and other plucked instruments in Morocco play, not chords, but melodies, while in Andalucía the guitar prefers, not melodies, but chords. Barbarous chords, it used to be said. Falla soon convinced me that they were a marvellous revelation of harmonic possibilities hitherto unsuspected.

The different kinds of song and dance heard in the south of Spain have their own special preludes, with effects of rhythm and harmony (particularly cross-accent and false relation) peculiar to each; but a good player, while keeping within the limits proper to the song or dance he is accompanying, will employ considerable variation, and a master like Barrios can vary his preludes indefinitely. Though I heard him every day for weeks on end, I never grew tired of his playing; and Falla, though he can hear that kind of playing all the year round, can always find something in it to interest him. Even to Falla the guitar is still full of unsuspected possibilities; while to a mere traveller the prelude to a *fandango* is always an electrifying experience.

The prelude lasts until the singer considers that the emotion of the audience (and the performer) has been sufficiently worked up; then the voice comes in with a long " *Ay!* " or " *Lelí, lelí,* " [2] followed by the characteristic wavering melody, punctuated at certain places by chords on the guitar and followed, at the end of each verse, by a recapitulation of the prelude.

The most striking feature of southern Spanish song of this kind is the characteristic cadence: la, sol, fa, mi. The melodies of the *fandango* and its derivatives, *malagueñas, rondeñas, granadinas,* etc., as well as the older *soleares, polos, seguidillas* and the rest — the chief exception (as far as I could determine) being the oldest of all, the *siguiriya gitana,* " gipsy

[2] See above, p. 25; i.e., the singer begins by unconsciously reciting the Muslim creed, or a vague memory of it.

42

seguidilla"—seem all to move in a harmonic atmosphere depending upon this "Phrygian" cadence, ending on what is apparently the dominant, which the guitar emphasizes in a way that leaves no doubt as to the effect intended. The *soleá* from Falla's opera *La Vida Breve* (*Life is Short*) is a good example, a movement entirely in the popular style.

Plenty of other instances may be found in Falla's music: in the ballet *El Amor Brujo*, for instance, in the first song; in the *polo* in the collection of *Seven Spanish Songs*, and in various dances in *The Three-Cornered Hat*. It is a cadence which has a long history, since it occurs in the earliest guitar versions of the Spanish (and Portuguese) *folías*, on which Corelli afterwards wrote his celebrated variations; in the accompaniment to *Las Vacas*, upon which lute-players and organists performed countless variations in the sixteenth century; and it was evidently a special favourite with Morales, who introduces it not infrequently into his church-music. It occurs on several occasions also in the harpsichord music of Domenico Scarlatti.[3] One instance may be quoted; and it is of especial interest, because Scarlatti has followed the characteristic la, sol, fa, mi, of southern Spain with three bars of pure guitar-music, showing the "internal pedal-point" (doubled, in this case) which is so striking in much of Falla's music, and, as we have seen, probably arose in popular music to

[3] See Chapter II.

43

suit the convenience of the guitar-player, by steadying his hand while changing other notes in the chord or arpeggio.

(Ed. Longo, Vol. I, No. 14)

Passages from a gavotte of Scarlatti also show the internal pedal-point, clearly suggested by the

(Ed. Longo, Vol. II, No. 58.)

guitar, and other instances may be found, some of which are illustrated in *Music and Letters* for April 1922 and the *Musical Quarterly*, 1927. The beginning of the Scherzo of Debussy's quartet is also a piece of music which Falla pronounced to be "very Andaluz in spirit"; and the reason, when one comes to look at it, may be that although the key-signature is G major, the theme apparently centres about the dominant of C minor. There is no definite phrase upon which one can put one's finger and say: "That is Andaluz," but the Andaluz feeling is certainly there.

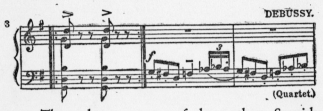

DEBUSSY.

(Quartet.)

These, then, are some of the southern Spanish qualities which either are exhibited in Falla's music or help to explain it. They refer to the letter rather than to the spirit; but the letter of the music is, perhaps, all that we can ever hope to understand about it; the spirit must be *felt*. It is (Falla declares) a mistake to think that music must be understood before it can be enjoyed. Music is not made to be understood, but to be felt. "*La música*," he said, "*no se hace para que se comprenda, sino para que se sienta.*" This perhaps is not the whole truth; and many might prefer the author of *Terpander*, when he states that "We do not enjoy music as an art until we have learned to appreciate it rationally; but at the same time it cannot give us a real æsthetic emotion unless it confronts us forcibly with a further irrational element."

One can be certain, however, what should be the attitude of a foreigner towards the music of southern Spain. What we have to do is to try to feel it — and, if possible, to play it — like a Spanish musician. There are times when I quite agree with those who say that they are tired of " the Spanish idiom," occasions when I hear a capable or even brilliant pianist playing Granados or Albéniz in London and in some curious way missing the point. They get all the notes, which is by no means an easy thing to do; they pedal and phrase quite nicely; they even play with a certain sense of design and get their climaxes in the right place. Yet something is wrong; and in Spain sometimes a wretched pianist playing at a third-floor window behind the flowerpots on the balcony will hold you and keep you standing in the street for so long that the neighbours begin to think that you are interested in other things than music and have come as a *pretendiente* for the lady's hand.

The feeling for southern Spanish music lies partly, of course, in a feeling for southern Spanish rhythms. Albéniz, Granados, Turina, Pérez Casas, Conrado del Campo, Oscar Esplá, and, most of all, Falla have an intense feeling for rhythmic effects. The scores of Falla's *Nights in the Gardens of Spain* and *The Three-Cornered Hat* are textures of conflicting rhythms; and the fact that Falla knows so well what it is to hear the transparent clearness of a trio of " twangling " instruments, and to write for it, leads him to handle the orchestra in something the same clear and transparent way. The trio of guitar, *laúd*, and *bandurria*, as was suggested above, gives a new idea of music and suggests that counterpoints

46

of both rhythm and melody can be made to sound, and to make their effect, in a way which would be impossible on a pianoforte or with a string quartet.

Experience with plucked instruments affects the rhythmic sense of a Spanish musician in another way. In the North we can all feel the rhythmic effect of chords on the violin. The chords in Bach's sonatas for violin solo, and in the best old Italian violin-music, are deliberately placed at points where a slight catch in the rhythm is necessary. If anyone tried to sing Bach's *Chaconne* or the slow movement from Tartini's Sonata in G minor (*Didone abbandonata*), it would sound meaningless unless he did something to suggest the appoggiatura effect of the big chords across the strings. It might be said, in fact, that the real object of chords on the violin is not so much to fill in the harmony or suggest the counterpoint as to produce a definite effect of rhythm.

Pianists who are not Spaniards, when they play the *Iberia* or the *Goyescas* or Falla's *Four Spanish Pieces*, his *Fantasía bética*, or transcriptions of the dances from *The Three-Cornered Hat*, generally forget that at the back of the composer's mind is a plucked instrument, the chords of which invariably give the effect of an appoggiatura and produce a vital throb in the rhythm. The effect of it might be compared with the habit of ladies in some out-of-the-way parts of Spain who have given up curtsying (to foreigners, at any rate), but who do it mentally so

47

that it gets into the rhythm of the first words they say to you.

Falla (whose full name is Manuel de Falla y Matheu) was born at Cádiz on the 23rd November 1876. His father was of Valencian extraction. Falla is a Valencian surname, and his forefathers came from Borja (or Borgia), near Gandía. His mother, as the name Matheu would imply, was a native of Catalonia. Falla therefore represents a blend of two different traditions: the imagination, grace, and humour of the Andaluz, and the clear-headedness, subtlety, and sense of form of the Mediterranean. His music is superficially Andaluz, but the clarity and directness of his thought is Mediterranean. To anyone from the south of Spain the music of his earlier manner is immediately intelligible, or at any rate strikes a chord in the memory and connects itself with something which has been heard before. A musician from Barcelona finds that although the turns of phrase belong to that Andaluz manner which, to him, is something exotic, Falla's music has a clearness and precision, a sense of order and arrangement, a reasonableness, which he would call the expressive Catalan word: "*seny.*" It is (as Professor Santayana would say) both inspiring to the imagination and inevitable to the understanding.

Falla's conversation shows the same double influence. There was an afternoon at Madrid, after a concert performance of Ravel's *Daphnis et Chloë,*

48

during which we had stood up at the back of a box looking over the full score; there were occasions while he was house-hunting at Granada when we sat drinking coffee and watching the sun set; and numberless other occasions since these notes were first written down, in 1922. Falla would launch out into a harangue about music, passionate and yet reasoned, outwardly all excitement and a flood of words, but inwardly as clearly thought out as a text-book. His talk is not always easy to follow, either in Spanish or in French. One has to see and hear a good deal of him before getting accustomed to the turn of his expression and the run of his thought; and those who have had only casual conversations with him (in French) are apt to carry away a mistaken idea of the man and his aims.

One day at Granada while we were lunching in the garden together under a quince-tree, the conversation turned upon Cádiz, and Falla spoke of his early life there. Cádiz, he explained, had a long musical tradition, and above all a long tradition for private music. In the eighteenth century, when it was still one of the most prosperous cities in the world, Italian opera companies came regularly from Madrid, and probably by sea as well, from Lisbon and elsewhere. People also learnt music by making it for themselves in their own homes. They sang Italian chamber-cantatas, they played string trios for two violins and a bass; and the bass, which Corelli and others directed to be played on the bass-viol, arch-lute, or harpsichord, was often played on the guitar. Cultivated music was entirely Italian, as it was all over Europe; and even characteristically Spanish works like *tonadillas* were influenced both in design and in melodic structure by the forms prevailing in Italy. Later in the century Boccherini came to Spain, bringing the fashion of Haydn; and a canon of the Church of La Cueva in the Calle del Rosario at Cádiz was able to commission Haydn to write his beautiful quartet-interludes to the " Seven Words from the Cross," which are still performed on Good Friday in the dark, subterranean church, to the uncertain glimmer of a few candles. (They are now also performed in the Cathedral at Cádiz, and at Seville.)

Thirty or forty years ago the custom of making music at home still prevailed at Cádiz; and Falla's earliest musical experiences came from chamber-music. With the exception of *The Seven Words from the Cross,* the music played and sung in church left no impression on him. His first public appearance, at the age of nine, was in the Church of San Francisco, playing *The Seven Words* as a duet with his mother, who was a talented pianist. The chamber-music which he heard, and in which he took part, was generally played at the house of an amateur 'cellist, who, with no great gift for music, had plenty of enthusiasm and got through a good deal of music.

Falla's earliest idea of music, then, was derived from a pianoforte trio or quartet, or a small orches-

tra; and the notion of what can be done with an
orquestilla is always at the back of his mind. It was
accident, perhaps, and the fact that they were first
performed in small theatres, that caused the earlier
versions of his two ballets to be arranged for something like a double quartet. But his interest in the
trio of outdoor instruments, and the scoring of the
Harpsichord Concerto, show that the feeling for a
small orchestra has persisted.

The influence on Falla of the teaching of Pedrell has already been remarked. The turning-point
in his career was, as he always insists, his journey to
Paris and meeting with Debussy in 1907. It has been
already suggested that Debussy wrote music which
was extremely Andaluz in spirit, without necessarily
using anything which could strictly be called
local colour; and, strange as it may seem, it was
Debussy who revealed things in the spirit of Andaluz
music which had been hidden or not clearly
discerned even by Falla, who was born and bred in
Andalucía.

Falla, so far (he arrived in Paris, as we have said,
with the finished score of *La Vida Breve*), had expressed the letter rather than the spirit of southern
Spanish music. So, at least, he felt after making the
personal acquaintance of Debussy; and in the "Debussy number" of the *Revue musicale* (December
1920) he explained what he considered that Debussy
had done for Spanish music. The article should be

read in his own words, as they were hammered out through several autumn mornings near the Alhambra. It is to be wished that editors of musical periodicals would not distract composers by leading them into the temptations of journalism — for, though in this case the result justified the time spent, Falla confessed that with less trouble and more dispatch he could have written a perfectly formal sonata. Debussy (he says) wrote Spanish music without knowing more of Spain — of the actual country, that is — than could be seen in a few hours spent at San Sebastian. He knew it, of course, from books, and from the songs and dances given by Spanish performers in Paris. Moreover, he was interested in the modal melodies of liturgical music; and as Spanish popular song has been influenced by the Church modes, it happened that even in the works of Debussy which were not intended to give a Spanish effect Falla met with the modal writing, together with the cadences, rhythms, and ornaments which seemed to bear a close relationship with the natural music of his own country.

Debussy's Andalucía was an Andalucía of dreams, like Mr. Walter de la Mare's " Arabia "; and to Debussy, Falla must have seemed like a visitor from his own dream-land. But if Debussy heard from Falla that his dreams had in a sense come true, Falla must have felt that he himself was, as it were, part of Debussy's dream — that he held the keys and knew the facts of those regions which Debussy knew only in imagination. Many of Debussy's works created a marvellous atmosphere of poetry and suggestion; to Falla these came with the force of an *evocación* of his own country and its music, and all his later work (down to *The Puppet-Show* and the Harpsichord Concerto) may be regarded as an effort to convey this poetry and suggestiveness with the conviction of one who knows that dreams can sometimes come true. So far he had been expressing the letter of Andaluz music; he began now to realize how Debussy had managed to convey the spirit.

It is not easy to find in Falla the direct traces of Debussy's influence which can be found in Albéniz; while in Albéniz's *Iberia* there are pieces which seem entirely pre-Debussy, although the collection was published after Debussy's orchestral suite of the same name. The earliest published compositions of Falla date from the year 1909, the year in which Albéniz died. They include the four *Pièces espagnoles pour le piano.* Three songs to words by Théophile Gautier were published in the following year. " *Andaluza,*" the last of the four pieces for the piano, is interesting to study, for it foreshadows Falla's later manner, while in its technique and its difficulties of execution it recalls Domenico Scarlatti; it is modern in conception and full of the spirit of southern Spain. As a kind of trio the composer has introduced a melody suggestive of *cante hondo,* and supported it by an internal pedal-point, something after the manner of Domenico Scarlatti.

Debussy's free rhythms, his modes, his snatches of melody which end on the dominant, and his passages resembling *cante hondo,* all suggest the atmosphere of the southern Spanish " Arabia." But of all his works, that which comes to a Spanish musician most charged with emotion is *" La Soirée dans Grenade."* The poetry and *evocación* concentrated in these few pages are overwhelming. This (Falla declares) is the real musical Andalucía; and although there is not a bar which is directly borrowed from Spanish popular music, the whole piece, down to the smallest details, has the feeling of Spain. The vague, wandering melody is not really *cante hondo,* but a poetical suggestion of it, an *evocación.* In structure it is pure Debussy, and so are the fragments reminiscent of *cante hondo* in the *Préludes: " La Puerta del Vino"* (Book II, No. 3) and *"La Sérénade interrompue"* (Book I, No. 9). This last prelude is, of

course, consciously "Spanish" in the witty style of
Gautier's "*Voyage*." It is full of deliberate guitar-
effects; one of the guitars, tuned in flats and playing
in B flat minor, being interrupted by another thrumming in D major. It is an illustration of what Calderón held to be the eleventh commandment: Thou
shalt not interrupt. The southern feeling in the
"*Soirée*" (and also in the "*Puerta del Vino*") is
intensified by the delightful *tango*—for that is what
the *habanera* really is; and the rhythm of it holds
both of these pieces together.

Debussy (Falla concludes) wrote "Spanish"
music, not by using authentic tunes, but by "feeling"
them, by realizing the foundations on which they rest
and conveying the essence of them in music which
was all his own. This (he thinks) is the way in which
folk-music is most satisfactorily treated by cultivated
musicians. It is true that his own *Seven Spanish Songs*
are genuine Spanish tunes; but their interest (as in
the folk-songs set by Vaughan Williams) lies not
only in the melodies, but also in the accompaniments
provided for them, which (in both cases) are entirely
suitable to the melodies, but at the same time entirely
personal to the composers.

The last work of Falla to be mentioned in this
chapter is the *Homenaje* for guitar, written for the
Debussy number of the *Revue musicale* and finished
soon after we reached Granada in the autumn of
1920. It is an extraordinary work (especially when

55

compared with the frivolity of some of the other compositions sent to deck the tomb of Debussy), full of that passionate seriousness which is characteristic of Falla's music and of all things which are really and truly Spanish. Falla's affection for the French master is beyond a doubt; so is the brusque gesture with which, by a recollection of " *La Soirée dans Grenade*," he tries to forget his grief. Its grimness is indescribable, and it is written for that despised instrument, the guitar.

CHAPTER IV

LA VIDA BREVE

La Vida Breve (*Life is Short* or *Our Little Life*) is the earliest of Falla's works which has survived. It was written in 1904 and 1905 and won a prize offered by the Real Academia de Bellas Artes in Madrid. It was not performed, however, and the composer started for Paris with the score in his bag — his passport to the society of Debussy and Dukas. The first performance took place at the Casino Municipal at Nice (1st April 1913). It was repeated at the Opéra Comique, Paris (30th December 1913); the first performance in Spain was given at the Teatro de le Zarzuela, Madrid, a year later (14th November 1914). It is comparatively short — about the length of the operas familiarly known to English singers as "Cav." and "Pag." — and would make a welcome change from either of these. It is rather uncertain in style, but the orchestration is extremely effective, and on the stage it succeeds far better than would be imagined from reading the pianoforte score. What particularly give it life are the interludes of Andaluz song and dance and the snatches of melody sung by voices "off." The work has a great sense of climax and would be well worth doing in England, although it would be impossible without expert professional Spanish advice.

The plot is of the slightest and has hardly given the composer a chance; indeed it might almost be suspected that Falla accepted it out of pure goodness of heart towards an otherwise talented poet and fellow townsman, the late Carlos Fernández Shaw. Salud, a gipsy girl of Granada, is deserted by her lover, Paco. She watches the wedding-feast through the iron railing, bursts with her family into the courtyard where the dance is being held, and falls dead at the faithless man's feet. An event of almost everyday occurrence, some might think, and yet, as Mr. Pedro Morales has acutely observed, Salud and not Carmen is the true Spanish type.

How is one to approach *La Vida Breve*? By what standard is one to judge it? It is childish to assume, as a French writer has assumed, that musical drama is not in the Spanish nature. The foundations of Spanish opera may be obscure, but when they have been excavated as thoroughly as have the foundations of English opera by Professor E. J. Dent, it will be seen that there is a Spanish sense of musical drama no less than an English one, though it may not be the same as that of France or Italy. Mario Castelnuovo-Tedesco, who critizes the opera from an Italian standpoint,[1] finds that *La Vida Breve*, although composed

---

[1] *Il Pianoforte*, IV, i (January 1923), pp. 8–17.

before Falla ever went to France, recalls French opera of the pre-Debussy period; not in the poetical part, which is extremely personal and characteristic, but in the handling of the dramatic situations. If the characters sometimes sing in the manner of Andaluz popular song, they more often approach that conception of lyric opera of which Massenet was the typical exponent, although it is Massenet in his better moments. From this point of view, Paco and Salud belong rather to French melodrama than to Spain; while Spanish music-drama is limited to the symphonic episodes, to the songs of the *cantaor* who sings at the wedding, and above all to those mysterious voices which are heard through the beating of hammers in a neighbouring forge in the first scene of Act I.

There's a lass ____ that's hard as i - ron,
Keep her cold, and she'll re - sist ____ thee;
Melt her in the fire, She's thine! ____

Mi querer es como el hierro:
se resiste con el frío
y se ablanda con el fuego.

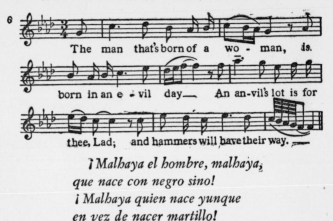

¡ Malhaya el hombre, malhaya,
que nace con negro sino!
¡ Malhaya quien nace yunque
en vez de nacer martillo!

The monologues of Salud, again, are intensely characteristic, though not one of them is an authentic folk-song:

¡*Vivan los que ríen!*
¡*Mueran los que lloran!*
La vía[2] *del pobre, que vive sufriendo,*
debe ser mu *corta.*

Flow-ers that blow__ of a morn-ing
ear-ly are dead when the day is done.__
Hap-py, hap-py are the flow-ers__ that
hard-ly live their life long enough to know the
pain__ that life__ is.__

Flor que nace con el alba
se muere al morir el día.
¡*Qué felices son las flores,*
que apenas puén *enterarse*
de lo malo que es la vía.

The strophic songs succeed in their purpose better
than the prose declamation. Later, in *The Puppet-
Show*, Falla was to achieve something new and personal, in a declamation which has caught the exact

---

[2] Following the Spanish custom, the dialect words are distinguished by type (via, *vida*; mu, *muy*; puén, *pueden*).

tone and inflection of Spanish speech; here, in *La Vida Breve*, he is faced with the same problem as Vaughan Williams in *Hugh the Drover*: how to adapt the strophic, folk-song form to dramatic speech — a problem which neither Falla nor Vaughan Williams was completely able to solve.

The truth seems to be that *La Vida Breve* suffers from an infirmity common among operas of all ages: at dramatic moments the vehicle of expression is the orchestra rather than the voices. This is due not to lack of technique, but to lack of experience. " The thematic treatment in the episodes independent of the drama, the symphonic movements illustrative of the sunset over Granada, the wedding-party, and others, have a sense of design and a vocal, melodic character which is treated firmly and expanded with ease and certainty; it is rather in the setting to music of dramatic situations that the composer's hand may seem to some critics to falter."

Yet for all the simplicity of the story, the situation was not a particularly easy one to handle. If Salud is in earnest in her lyrical outburst on the arrival of Paco, the music of Paco himself must convey to the audience (though not to Salud) the feeling that he is pretending and that his protestations are insincere. Mozart would have made this clear, and so would Verdi and Wagner; but it is a difficult problem for a young composer in his first opera, unsupported by a strong national operatic tradition. The nearest we get to it is that insincerity is expressed in the manner of Massenet, and faith in manner of folk-song, and that insincerity can impose upon faith to such an extent that when both are present at the same time (as in the passionate and effective duet between Paco and Salud in the first act), it is the music of insincerity which dominates everything with its apparent seriousness. In the second act the position is reversed — or apparently reversed. Salud, standing in the street, gazing through the bars of the *reja* at the wedding-dance going on in the courtyard, abandons the folk-song manner, which has been taken up, in a popularized, thoughtless way by the dancers inside. It is they who are in the " right," or on the right side; Salud who is in the " wrong."

Her grandmother and old uncle Salvador *(Tío Sarvaor)* persuade her to go in, and the three present themselves as gipsy musicians, ready to dance and sing.

Among the chattering guests, Manuel, the host, is heard asking them what they want.

" What a sight! . . . What do you want here? "

(" Look what gipsies! What a fine girl! ")

" Would you kindly tell us why . . . ?"

" Isn't there a dance? Isn't there a wedding? " says Uncle Salvador. " We can dance; we can sing."

(" What can they want here? " Paco asks himself.)

" What, old man, you dance with legs like that? "

"I dance; I sing like a nightingale; and she—
this little girl — can sing better than a canary."

"I don't!" Salud cries suddenly.

"Child!"

"What does she say?"

("Holy God!")

"No, no! I have not come to sing! I have not
come to dance! I have come to see this . . . traitor!
To tell him, for God's sake, to kill me. Let him finish
with me, put an end to me, murder me!"

A moment after, she drops dead, and the sordid,
pitiful story is over. The background of thoughtless
dance-music has given place to tragedy, in which we
hear fragments of the folk-song sung in the forge.

> The man that's born of a woman
> Is born in an evil day,
> An anvil's lot is for thee, lass. . . .

Salud has sung the tune too$_2$ and applied it to
herself.

CHAPTER V

THE NOCHES

The three Nocturnes for orchestra and piano-forte, *Noches* (nights) *en los jardines de España,* were the first works in which Falla gave the true measure of his power as a composer. They were finished in 1916 and eventually reached London in 1921, being played by the composer himself at one of the concerts of contemporary music conducted by Mr. Edward Clark.[1] Among the many works given at those concerts which have not outlived the fashion of the hour — the program included a number of works by the French " Six," too expressive of the mood of the Armistice to make it possible to listen to them now — Falla's Nocturnes stood out as serious, genuine music, and the audience at the Queen's Hall, though it will applaud most new things out of

[1] This was not, as has sometimes been stated, Falla's first appearance in England. He played in London in 1911 (24th May) at one of the concerts organized by the late Franz Liebich, giving his *Four Pieces for the Piano,* accompanying songs by Turina and himself, and joining with Franz Liebich in a performance of Debussy's *Iberia,* arranged for two pianos by André Caplet. The program also included two sets of variations *(diferencias)* by the sixteenth-century composer Antonio de Cabezón.

politeness, does not often break into cheers, as it did on this occasion. The audience was roused not only by the music itself, and by the sense of security and conviction that belong to a masterpiece, but also by the composer's own performance, which was masterly, though concealed by a modesty which led some hearers to believe that the Nocturnes might be improved, or made still more interesting, by being played by one of the recognized *prime donne* of pianoforte-playing. Yet this is not so. Played under such conditions, the Nocturnes become a piano concerto, which is not at all what the composer intended them to be. In difficulty they are certainly comparable to a piano concerto; but the position of the pianoforte in the texture of the work, and the balance between it and the rest of the orchestra, are not those of a piano concerto, as that form is usually understood. The pianoforte is here an instrument of the orchestra, which, though it has passages of outstanding difficulty and brilliance, yet remains a part of the orchestra itself.

The *Noches* are not a concerto, and they are not program-music. On that point the composer is definite. "If," he says, "these 'symphonic impressions' have achieved their object, the mere enumeration of their titles should be a sufficient guide to the hearer. Although in this work — as in all which have a legitimate claim to be considered as music — the composer has followed a definite design, regarding

tonal, rhythmical, and thematic material . . . the end
for which it was written is no other than to evoke [the
memory of] places, sensations, and sentiments. The
themes employed are based (as in much of the composer's earlier work) on the rhythms, modes, cadences,
and ornamental figures which distinguish the popular
music of Andalucía, though they are rarely used in
their original forms; and the orchestration frequently
employs, and employs in a conventional manner, certain effects peculiar to the popular instruments used in
those parts of Spain. The music has no pretensions to
being descriptive: it is merely expressive. But something more than the sounds of festivals and dances
has inspired these 'evocations in sound,' for melancholy and mystery have their part also."

The orchestra employed in the *Noches* is large
—larger than Falla has used in any other of his works.
It comprises:

   2 flutes, piccolo, 2 oboes, English horn, 2 clarinets,
      2 bassoons.
   4 horns, 2 trumpets, 3 trombones, and tuba.
   3 drums, triangle, cymbals, celesta, harp, piano-
      forte, strings.

Falla begins in a way that is highly characteristic
of him: that is, directly, with no beating about the
bush. Tentative, hesitating beginnings are part of
the luggage belonging to the romantic period which
contemporary composers discard, and Falla with them.

In the *Noches* we wake suddenly into the middle of a vivid dream, as if the music had been there already, going on for some time, before we became aware of it. We hear a buzzing tune for violas — rapidly repeated notes played close to the bridge, picked out and supported by the harp, and reinforced on the first beat of the bar by soft chords on strings and brass.

When the pianoforte enters, it is with an inversion of the theme supported by decorative arpeggios, and by clarinets, horns, and muted trumpets.

After some time another theme is suggested by the full orchestra:

and immediately afterwards taken up and developed by the pianoforte, once again in an inverted form:

one of those quasi-oriental melodies which seem to go on for ever, and yet (when we come to listen carefully) it turns out to be a regular eight-bar tune. After the orchestra has repeated its (uninverted) version of the tune in the relative major, the music gradually becomes stilled.

It is marked *poco calmo,* but it is a tense, not tragic, stillness; and after a short cadenza for the pianoforte (against which reminiscences of the opening theme are heard softly on the strings) a theme gradually emerges from it, which leads us back to the opening, the rapidly repeated notes this time being played on the pianoforte in a manner highly characteristic of Falla's way of writing for that instrument. At the end, in a short coda, the original theme is recalled by the horn — repeated in augmentation — *pp marcato* (a favourite direction of Falla's) against a still softer background of strings.

This first movement has been called after the Generalife — *jannat al-'arîf,* " the garden of the architect " (or the musician) — on a hill-side overlooking the Alhambra, the most beautiful place in the whole of Granada. The second piece is described as " *Danza lejana* (A Dance in the Distance)," and once again we wake to find it in full swing. An exciting trill and run is being played by a few violas, supported by 'cellos and basses *pizzicato.*

They are soon joined by flute and English horn;

and then, with the same persistent rhythm going on at the back, two flutes come forward, with the following played in thirds:

The pianoforte then enters with the figure introduced by the flute and English horn:

the rhythm which accompanies it in the right hand
being heard a good deal as the dance progresses.
Another quasi-oriental tune is played by flute and
strings:

and immediately repeated by English horn, clarinet,
and 1st violins; while flute, piccolo, and oboe return to
the trill and run originally heard on the violas. Against
these we hear the rhythm persisting in the pianoforte;
and from the harp, chords suggesting the sound of a
guitar.

The persistent rhythm now passes to the strings,
while the horns give out a version of No. 5, which
we now see to be an augmentation of the rhythm in
the bass.

The pianoforte then takes the melody, until at last
the rhythm breaks away in the basses:

and dominates the dance, appearing in various combinations, such as

until the moment arrives for a change of scene. This
Falla describes as follows: "The second and third
nocturnes are joined without interruption by means
of a bridge in which, beneath a tremolo on the violins
in the highest register, are sprinkled, like distant
echoes, the notes which begin the fundamental theme
of the 'Distant Dance.' The bridge ends with an as-
cending passage for the pianoforte, in octaves, which
is resolved in a *tutti* with which the third and last
nocturne begins."

The last nocturne is called "In the gardens of the Sierra de Córdoba." We have suddenly been transported to one of those large villas on the hill-side above Córdoba, on an evening when a party is in progress, with a *zambra* of gipsy musicians: players, singers and dancers, while somewhere under the trees is a long trestle table with a row of *dama-juanas* (demi-johns) holding two or three firkins of manzanilla apiece.

The word *zambra* tempts one to a short philological digression, a digression which may not be altogether out of place if it helps to put us in the mood of the music. The word *sâmira* was used by the Moors in Spain for revelry by night, or even for a quiet nocturnal meeting at which a number of people passed the night together telling stories, like those of the *Thousand and One Nights*. But as no real *sâmira* was complete without music and dancing, the word came also to be used for a band of musicians. Even that inhuman monk Cardinal Ximénez, the greatest enemy of the Spanish Muslims (who tried to destroy in one day the culture of seven centuries, by burning every Arabic manuscript which could be found in Granada) — even Ximénez liked what he called *zambras* to accompany the sacrament during the processions at Corpus Christi, " where were gathered together all the villages in rivalry one with another as to who should bring the best *zambra*." And in the mountains of the Alpujarra near Granada, when the Cardinal made a visitation, he found that for mass, instead of organs, of which they had none, music was made by the *zambras*. " I remember," says an eyewitness, " that when, during mass, the parish priest turned to the people, instead of ' *Dominus vobiscum* ' he would say: ' May Allah bless you ' in colloquial Arabic, and then the *zambra* would respond." (The derivation is also said to be from the Arabic *zamara*, to play on a wind instrument: the " b " has come into the word through the same phonetic law which changed *al-hamrâ*, " the red," into Alhambra, and *ramla*, " a sandy lane," into the magnificent Ramblas of Barcelona.) Gradually, as the persecution of the Moriscos increased during the sixteenth century, their *zambras* were prohibited; Philip II ordered that the Moriscos should neither have nor hold *zambras* or *leylas* (nights), with instruments or Moorish songs. But he had forgotten to reckon with the gipsies, who began to arrive in Granada about the time that the Moriscos began to be driven out; and the gipsies, though they were incapable of the industry and craftsmanship of the Moriscos, yet preserved something of their manner of performing music.

For the third of Falla's Nocturnes, then, we may
have in our minds an evening party at a villa near
Córdoba, where a band of gipsy musicians has been
engaged as a normal and necessary part of the entertainment. Their music is wild to the last degree —
wild, and repeated again and again:

with utterly unexpected climaxes:

and perverse noises on the brass:

76

and snatches of the characteristic *cante andaluz* or *cante hondo* (see pages 19 et seq.).

A dancer is present also, and soon she comes out, with her stamping on the ground, and sudden holding of a turn or a gesture:

The characteristic rhythm hesitating between 6/8 and 3/4 is not forgotten, while the music is characteristically marked "*incisivo e sonoro, ma non forte,*" a direction which applies generally to a good deal of Falla's music:

They keep it up till morning (the music seems to say), till the feet and limbs of the dancers almost begin to tire and the fingers and wrists of the guitar-players almost to lose their rhythm. It has been a wild night, orgiastic, un-European; and yet the composer has so arranged things that we have it all clearly before us, and our dreams do not outstay their vividness. Falla's art lies in this: that he has made it seem not exotic, but natural. We have been caught up, like Christopher Sly, like the Prince in Calderón's play of *Life's a Dream*, or like The Sleeper Wakened in the *Arabian Nights*, to hear things and to see things with other senses than ours, and yet with senses that all the time are our own. It was a dream, but at the same time it was real.

CHAPTER VI

EL AMOR BRUJO

The name of the gipsy ballet *El Amor Brujo* has never been satisfactorily translated. *Brujo* means a wizard, a male witch; and the French " *L'Amour sorcier* " has misled both audiences and English translators. *Love the Wizard* gives an entirely wrong impression; *Wedded by Witchcraft,* proposed as an alternative, is a description, more or less, of what happens; and even that would be better as *Wedded in spite of Witchcraft.* Remembering the Border ballad, we might suggest the name of *The Demon Lover,* except that the story is different, or put into other words the name of Dvořák's cantata, *The Spectre's Bride.* This is the name which best describes what happens. The story is derived from the folk-tale, found from Cornwall to Czecho-Slovakia, in which the ghost of the dead lover always appears at the moment when a new lover tries to take his place. It seems to be connected with the story of " the Ring given to Venus," or, in early Spanish poems and French miracles, to the Virgin Mary. The lover had slipped a ring on the finger of a statue in church, believing it to be that of

the Virgin, but the statue had originally been one of
Venus. The finger bent and kept the ring, and the
statue always appeared in person to prevent the con-
summation of an earthly marriage.

Falla's ballet (the scenario of which is by
Martínez Sierra) shows how "love lays the spectre"
— which might do for a translation — and the method
employed is, as might be imagined, that of dancing.

Candélas, a beautiful and passionate gipsy, was
once loved by another gipsy, a "tough" in every
sense of the word, a man of evil reputation, jealous
and dissolute, but one whom no woman could resist.
She had been unhappy with him as long as he lived,
but she mourned him and could not forget him. She
is still afraid of him; she believes that the dead man
is not quite dead, and that he may come back and
continue to love her in his old savage and faithless
fashion. Thoughts of the past prey upon her; she
feels herself entirely in the power of the man's ghost.
She is still young, however. Spring returns, and brings
a new lover in the shape of Carmélo.

Carmélo is young too, *beau garçon,* attentive,
very much in love. He presses his suit on Candélas,
who is ready to be convinced, if it were not for the
past, which is always there to hinder her present
happiness; and whenever Carmélo draws near, in
the hope that she may share his passion, the ghost
returns and frightens Candélas away from her lover.

Having refused Carmélo, Candélas seems to pine

away; she feels herself bewitched; memories of her
past love flit about her "like malevolent and fore-
boding bats." (This elegant expression is taken from
the "argument" printed in the score — a production
which is almost as curious an example of French prose
as the "Synopsis" is odd as a piece of English.) Something must be done, however, and Carmélo thinks
that he has found the remedy. He had known the man
whose ghost now haunts Candélas — a typical Andaluz, jealous and unfaithful; and as, even after his
death, women still seem to have an attraction for him,
he must be attacked at his weakest point, if jealousy
stronger than death is to be done away with.

So Carmélo persuades Lucía, a young friend of
Candélas, to allow the ghost to make love to her instead; and Lucía agrees, partly out of friendship for
Candélas and partly out of feminine curiosity. She
is on the look-out when Carmélo comes next day
to see Candélas; the ghost comes as well, but is confronted with Lucía, whom he finds irresistible. While
he is making love to her, Carmélo has time to con-
vince Candélas of his love; nature prevails, life vindi-
cates its rights over death and the past, and the lovers
fall into each other's arms, while the ghost is laid for
good and all.

The music to this ballet is often played as a suite,
with the numbers arranged in the wrong order. But
the music alone can give little idea of how effective, how overwhelming, the ballet is on the stage;

and if the audience has not seen it danced — or if the conductor has not seen it danced — there is little possibility of understanding the composer's intentions. When the rhythms can be seen as well as heard, and when they take plastic shape before the eyes, we realize what a masterpiece the work is.

The composer has kept the stage in his mind from beginning to end. Not only the rhythms, but the shapes of the phrases are all thought of in terms of the dance; and when these are interpreted by the greatest living Spanish dancer, the invisible movement of the music and the visible motions of the dance seem to be all one; the dance is a consequence of the music. This unity is preserved in the performances given by "La Argentina." A rehearsal by her is a marvellous object-lesson in how such a thing should be done. Given the music, with the proper *tempi* and the rhythms as the composer directs, La Argentina takes charge of all the rest. She knows exactly what she wants and how to get it. Not a detail escapes her. Every movement of her small corps-de-ballet, every effect of lighting, must be tried again and again until it is perfect. One of the dancers, for instance, may not be Spanish and may not move a certain portion of her anatomy exactly as a Spanish dancer would move it. She must go on trying until she does so. The lighting may not be up-to-date, even in Paris; La Argentina finds out exactly what can be done with the means at hand and then insists that it *shall* be done, every time, at exactly the right instant. The ghost must appear as if from nowhere. A moment ago he was not there. Three sighing chords for strings, followed by an agitated phrase for muted trumpet:

and there he stands—with a green, phosphorescent light on his unshaven chin, as if he had just come out of his grave and had brought his own glow-worms with him. There must be no suggestion of his "walking on" and being picked up afterwards by a green spotlight. These things must happen as if by magic—they must happen, that is, by *music*. Everybody concerned in the performance must make his or her own particular movements with the musicianship and inevitability of a trained dancer. *Then* we get a performance second to none and realize that, between them, Falla and La Argentina have created one of the greatest masterpieces of modern times.

The music dates from about 1915. That, at least,

was the year in which the work was first given, with
a small orchestra, at the Teatro de Lara in Madrid. It
had been in the composer's mind for some time before
and has had a certain small amount of revision since.
It is difficult (as Falla says himself) to give an
exact date for any of his works. It was printed in
1921 (Chester) in a pianoforte arrangement, and in
1924 in miniature score. It is Falla's greatest triumph
in the purely Spanish manner; it is music which anyone could recognize immediately as being Spanish,
because of the Andaluz "idiom" in which it is written. Critics, from the first, have classified it as folk
or "nationalistic" music. I have the best authority
— the composer's own — for stating that there is not
a single folk-tune in it, anywhere, from beginning
to end. The rhythms of Andalucian dance were running in his head, but there are no quotations.

As finally revised, *El Amor Brujo* is scored for
a normal theatre orchestra without trombones: two
flutes, piccolo, oboe, two clarinets, bassoon; two horns,
two trumpets; timpani and bells (a, d, e) ; pianoforte
and strings. The pianoforte has an important part,
but it is used throughout as an orchestral instrument.
A mezzo-soprano voice sings "behind" (generally
interpreted as "from the orchestra"), though in concert performances the voice is replaced either by a
horn or, in one place, by an English horn.

The importance of the rhythm has already been
pointed out. It is not that Falla depends on the purely

physical or nervous appeal of repeated rhythmic figures. He alternates and contrasts varied rhythms,
makes counterpoints of them, and plays off one
against the other. But the difficulty which some conductors experience is to make the rhythms articulate.
It is a question not of pace, but of clearness. Falla
takes endless pains to mark everything and leave
nothing to chance; and his interpreters have to distinguish clearly between the effects of notes marked
> and those with only —. His music requires, too,
as a rule, a definite accent on the first beat of the
bar. Anyone who is at all intimately concerned with
the production or rehearsal of one of these works will
find himself going about, grunting the rhythms not
altogether inaudibly, much as Beethoven is said to
have done when he went for a country walk. It is as
near the mind of Beethoven, perhaps, as any of us
are ever likely to get.

Examples of Falla's rhythmic effects and the
marks by which he distinguishes them are readily to
be found in the " Ritual Fire-dance " which has become popular as a pianoforte piece; and if all the

marks are carefully observed, the pianoforte can give
a very good idea of it. The dynamic expression of the
recurrent figure in the bass should be noticed.

Not one of those four notes has the same accent, and
the third has a much heavier accent than most pianists
and conductors ever give it. Again, the accented
triplet or the gradually increasing excitement of

33

should be marked in the detachment and strength of
accentuation of the repeated A's.

A thing which neither the pianoforte nor a concert performance can give, however, is the harsh,
piercing, barbaric cry of Candélas and her dancers,
first on the " off " beats and then on the " off " bars.
Listening to that in Paris, one feels the city crumble
to dust; to be non-existent, desert, sown with salt.
Where is the boasted *mundo latino*, the " Defence of

86

the West," or Europe itself? If Falla is Latin in this, he is like a Latin writer — Apuleius, for instance, author of *The Golden Ass* — using the Latin language to describe utterly un-Latin things. Away with sophistication! Here we get down to the beggarly elements; and the only "Latin" quality of Falla's music is that it has enabled us to see these things so clearly.

Candélas — or, rather, her disembodied voice in the orchestra — begins by singing a melancholy, meditative song, the *"Canción del amor dolido,"* heavily, and even oppressively, accompanied by strings. Then follow the three mysterious bars for strings already quoted, followed by the quick movement for pianoforte and repeated staccato notes on a muted trumpet, and we suddenly notice that the ghost is there. There follows a "Dance of Terror," after which the distracted Candélas draws a magic circle and begins to mutter incantations over a smoking cauldron, to the piece of music which, for some reason, has been called *" Récit du pêcheur."* Playing it over on the pianoforte can give no idea of the beauty of the scoring: two soft muted trumpets alternating with a short phrase for strings. Later on, the passage for muted trumpets is repeated by flutes, accompanied as before by pinging little appoggiaturas on the pianoforte. The two chords at the end sound like an *Amen;* but when the ballet is actually seen and not merely heard, we realize that La Argentina

87

has finished her magic and crosses herself — down for
the first bar and across for the second, while on the
pause she brings her closed hand to her lips, and
kisses the thumb, in the traditional manner.

The clock strikes twelve; Candélas prepares to
dance the "Ritual Fire-dance" already described,
that shall drive away all evil spirits. It is of no use;
the ghost comes back.

Then a voice is heard singing a "*Canción del
fuego fátuo*," a "Song of the Jack-o'-lantern": [1]

Lo mismo que er *fuego fátuo,*
lo mismito es el queré.

[1] In accordance with Spanish practice, the words in dialect are
distinguished by type.

Le juyes, *y te persigue,*
le yamas, *y echa á* corré.
                    Lo mismo . . .

¡ *Malhaya los ojos negros*
que le alcanzaron á ver!
¡ *Malhaya* er *corazón triste*
que en su llama quiso ardé!
                    Lo mismo . . .

Roughly translated, so as to fit the music, this would
read as follows:

Oh, this love's a Jack-o'-lantern,
Jack-o'-lantern is his way!

Then, alas, those black eyes flaming,
They saw Jack-o'-lantern play!
                    Oh, this love . . .

Alas for the heart that's sorrowful,
And burns in that flame alway,
                    Oh, this love . . .

The "Pantomime" that follows is notable for the
slow dance in 7/8 time. It is a real seven-beat movement, not a fake; but it is by no means so slow as
some conductors take it ($\eighthnote = 168$).

By this time Lucía has appeared to divert the
ghost's attention the next time he appears. The
"*Danza del juego de Amor*" begins:

35 Allegretto mosso ♩.=60.

and the mysterious voice is heard once more. The ghost is eventually overcome by the beauty of Lucía and her dancing, while Candélas and Carmélo are left to consummate their happiness without interruption. Again the voice is heard as in a prophecy:

36

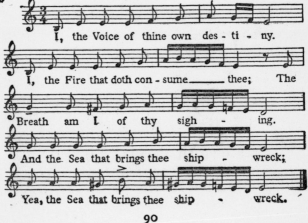

I, the Voice of thine own des - ti - ny.

I, the Fire that doth con - sume____ thee; The

Breath am I of thy sigh - ing.

And the Sea that brings thee ship - wreck;

Yea, the Sea that brings thee ship - wreck.

Soy la voz de tu destino,
Soy er fuego en que te abrasas,
Soy er viento en que suspiras,
Soy la mar en que naufragas,
Soy la mar en que naufragas.

The ghost is overcome and vanishes into thin air. His clothes are found by some of the dancers and brought in. The bells of morning are heard. . . .

We find ourselves standing up along with our neighbours, clapping our hands sore and shouting ourselves hoarse. La Argentina, recalled again and again, moves forward with her incomparable grace; she holds out her arms to Falla in the wings, but he steadily refuses to appear. The curtain descends for the last time; we rub our eyes and wonder where we are.

Do I dream, or have I dreamed till now?

No, we did not dream. It all happened so. The improbable, impossible story was true; it was made true by Falla's music and the interpretation of La Argentina.

CHAPTER VII

FANTASÍA BÉTICA

Grim and fantastic as the story of *El Amor Brujo* is, wild and barbaric as is the music, it has seemed not exotic, but natural — the natural expression of a natural course of events, and only the keenest sense of form and logic can make such music or such poetry seem that. Falla's music is the natural expression of people who live under those conditions; and they live in as natural a world — have as reasonable a soul "and human flesh subsisting" — as a Parisian audience. Live for some time in Granada, in touch with Spanish friends, and Spanish musical friends, and you find (unless you are a born Parisian) that it is not the music of Granada which sounds exotic, but the music of Paris; you can only tolerate those pieces of Debussy which seem by some means or other to have divined the Andaluz atmosphere. The rest seem not only exotic (as you feel them to be, listening to them in Granada), but artificial. The music of *El Amor Brujo* on the contrary, has a force and directness which make it immediately intelligible anywhere; and, moreover, it has the advantage of being unmistakably Spanish — of sounding "exactly what Spanish music is supposed to sound like."

Falla's last essay in this recognizably Spanish manner was the *Fantasía Bética* for pianoforte, written in 1919 and dedicated to Arthur Rubinstein. It is a work which has not been played as often as it ought to have been. Harmonically considered, it is the most uncompromising of all Falla's works; and many musicians, looking at the music without playing it, would think at once of certain effects of Stravinsky. Yet these things do not sound like Stravinsky at all; even the ninths near the end, when they come to be played, turn out to be pure Falla, and the rhythms are no less personal and characteristic. As is usual with Falla, we are plunged at once into a place in which a steady but relentless rhythm seems to have been going on already for a considerable time before we begin to hear it.

There is nothing frivolous about the *Fantasía;* the underlying idea is serious or even tragical; even the gay rhythm of the *sevillanas,* or *bolero,* and the rattle of a tambourine:

seems like a mocking laugh. Snatches of melody are repeated, in either the major or the minor, broadly and lyrically

or in the " chopstick " manner which Falla can make so effective:

We hear the guitar-player in his prelude (he must have transposed the instrument up a tone, as those who accompany *cante andaluz* frequently do, so that his B, E, A, and F♯ are all open strings):

94

We hear the singer (the *cantaor*) begin, on C♮, with his long "*Ay!*" followed by the first line of the *copla,* with a single chord on the guitar at the beginning and a rapid passage on the sustained notes. The theme of the song remains in the composer's head, where it undergoes a curious musical and psychological transformation:

95

Next comes a quiet and restful interval, an austere modal melody:

after which the main themes are recapitulated, and the *Fantasía* ends in a fashion thoroughly characteristic of Falla. It makes an interesting comparison with the *Homenaje (Homage)* in memory of Debussy, already referred to,[1] which was originally written for guitar and then arranged for pianoforte by the composer. Not only in technique and harmony, but in mood also, the two pieces are curiously alike — passionate utterances, in deadly earnest, yet controlled by a

[1] See page 63.

rigid logic and sense of form. And, regarded from another aspect, if the *Fantasía* represents the farthest that Falla has gone in adapting the harmonic peculiarities of the guitar to the modern pianoforte, the *Homenaje* — by no means ordinary, conventional, guitar-music — represents an attempt to make the guitar speak with the language of Falla.

For some time before this, carping critics in his own country had been saying that Falla was not writing Spanish music at all, but French — an accusation which is completely disproved and shown to have no foundation, by hearing any of his works in Paris, where nothing less " French " could well be imagined, indeed they are praised for their " exotic " local colour.

The exception — the only one of his later works which seems to have a Parisian feeling — is *Psyche,* a setting for voice and instruments (harp, flute, violin, viola, and 'cello) of a poem by M. Jean-Aubry. Falla's sense of language, his consciousness that, in their accentuation, French and Spanish are at opposite poles, is reflected in the structure and feeling of the music he has written for M. Jean-Aubry's words. Everything is vague and indirect; nothing is definitely stated; there is hardly a single common chord from beginning to end.

The reaction, when it came, was violent; it resulted in the *Soneto de Góngora,* the directness of which is almost too evident. Directness has always been a passion with Falla. He illustrated it one day to me by two examples from Spanish writers of the " golden century " — the beginning of one of the *Exemplary Novels* of Cervantes, where all is directness and clearness of vision, and the beginning of a story, or stories within a story, by Tirso de Molina — a pathless labyrinth of dependent clauses. Falla's conversion to Góngora came as a surprise to some of his friends. The usual idea of Góngora — one of the greatest of Spanish poets — is that of over-decorated unintelligibility, a writer to be dismissed unread with a play upon words, such as " Gongorism and Gorgonism." He died in 1627, the father of the baroque poetry of Europe; and in 1927 the best of the younger Spanish poets decided to do what they could to celebrate the tercentenary. Their task was the more grateful in that the Spanish Academy had officially decided not to recognize the event, while they themselves, unlike the Academicians, the detractors and critics of Góngora, had really read his works.

Falla was at first no friend to Góngora.[2] " To the invitations to join in the celebrations had succeeded an anxious silence. Falla, influenced no doubt by current ideas — unjust as they were — concerning Góngora, probably thought him dry and not really poetical *(poco espiritual)*. However, Lorca [one of

---

[2] *Carmen: revista chica de poesía española* (December 1927). *Lola: amiga y suplemento de Carmen.* No. 1 (Santander: Aldus S. A. de Artes Gráficas).

the best of the younger Spanish poets, and a great friend of Falla's] did not lose hope. One day he managed to get the *maestro* to read some of Góngora's letters in the edition of Foulché Delbosc. The day after, he found Falla steeped *(enfrascado)* in Góngora. 'Magnificent, magnificent! What a man! What greatness of spirit! What an artist! And look, just like our own artists! The same lack of compression for purity of line *(incompresiones para la pureza)*, for the firmness of their art!'

"By that time it was only a question of choosing the text: the *Soneto a Córdoba* written at Granada. Falla also dated his music from Granada. Góngora's verses will be sung gloriously all over the world! 'For Córdoba,' said Falla, 'is Roman; Roman as Góngora saw her, and not Arab. In the whole sonnet there is no allusion which is not Roman, Christian!' "

I give this account with all reserve, since Falla will admit the truth of no interview. But it is true that for some years the Roman idea of Andalucía has been taking possession of him, chiefly (I think) for artistic reasons — for the force and economy of expression, and for the permanence of Roman types among the country people of Southern Spain. He wishes to be Latin, to affirm his Latinity — not in the sense of the "Latin press," the "Latin world," or the "Latin genius" so belauded by certain newspapers — not in any modern sense of the word "Latin," but in the sense in which Latin stands among all the other languages. He would like his music to be, as it were, written in Latin; to be as economical and as expressive as Latin, with its grandeur, permanence, and universality, and he would doubtless consider — with the approval of certain philologists, not necessarily Spanish — that of all neo-Latin languages none has preserved the essential Latin qualities of concision and directness as Spanish has. French is too thin and penetrating, Italian too liquid and elastic, Portuguese (in modern days) too much dominated by nasal vowels and the sound of *sh*. Spanish may have a metallic ring, but it is the ring of bronze, a bronze copy of a Roman marble statue.

In the hands of Góngora the Spanish language became not bronze, but brass. The *Sonnet to Córdoba* should be declaimed through a brazen trumpet by a colossal marble angel on the façade of a baroque cathedral, and Falla's setting could only be completely convincing if it were sung by someone who could imagine herself to have, for a moment, the position and attributes of a baroque angel.

It was translated, somewhat inadequately and freely, by Archbishop Churton, the first biographer of Góngora, who, in the sixties of the last century, when no documents were available, wrote a life of the poet before anyone else in Europe had ever heard of him. The version published with the music by the Oxford University Press is closer to the original, although it does not read well, owing to the necessity of following the music exactly, so that, should occasion arise, the song may be sung to English words.

The poet is in Granada, but is thinking of his home, which was Córdoba. He remembers in imagination — with a good deal of imagination, the modern traveller would remark, if he has ever seen Córdoba itself — the "lofty bastions," the towers crowned with honour, majesty, and bravery; the great river, Guadalquivir (*wad' al-kabîr*, we remember, is, literally, "the great river"), the King of Andalucía, "whose sands are noble though their gold be wanting." Then he thinks of her fertile plains, the Sierra rising behind them, "which morn delights to gild and heaven to favour," his ever-glorious home.

Yet (he goes on) if among these ruins and spoils — that is, the Moorish palaces of the Alhambra — bathed by the rivers Genil and Darro, the memory of thee, Córdoba, be not my daily bread, never let my eyes, absent from home, deserve to see again thy walls, towers, and mountains, thy peaks and plains, my fairest country!

This is not narrow or local patriotism or a distortion of history. Every man writes as he must, and the result justifies the premises, both in words and music.

CHAPTER VIII

THE THREE–CORNERED HAT

The ballet of *The Three-Cornered Hat* was first performed in London on the 22nd July 1919, under Ansermet, at the Alhambra Theatre. Massine was the miller, Karsavina the miller's wife, Woizikovsky the *Corregidor*. It was the first of the ballets decorated by Picasso; and if there was at first some criticism of " an aimlessness in the movements of the crowds and an apparent monotony of rhythm . . . what there was for all the world to see was the delicate flickering beauty of the scene, the suggestion by a single masterly line here and there of hill or bridge, the faint stars silver in a silver-blue sky and the sun-bleached rose of the wall that told you of all the heat of that Southern village."[1]

From the musical point of view it was the last of the great ballets produced by the Diaghilev company, being followed by the rapid decline and fall which came with the "Armistice" style. And even now, when the "Armistice" style has been abandoned in the whole of Europe and America by all intelligent musicians, it still finds a home with the

[1] W. A. Propert: *The Russian Ballet in Western Europe* (1921), pp. 54–5.

music of the Diaghilev ballet, which few would go to see — or, rather, to hear as well as to see — if it were not that the program of every season included *The Three-Cornered Hat*. This may sound like an exaggeration; but the youngest and keenest members of a ballet audience are not old enough to remember the war and cannot understand what the Armistice was about, or the style of composition to which it gave birth; and serious students of the ballet — of dancing as well as of music — look no longer to Paris, but to Germany, where new ballets are given by directors like Laban and composers such as Honegger and Bartók, whose music is neither " Armistice " nor " Parisian Neo-Classic." The ballet had a function to perform, and down to 1920 it splendidly performed it; such pre-Diaghilev performances as the French ballet's interpretation of Ravel's *Daphnis et Chloë* at the International Festival of Contemporary Music at Frankfurt in 1927 enabled a large cosmopolitan audience to see how things had moved on since the arrival of the Russians. The post-Diaghilev style of ballet-music has now appeared in Germany and in Paris in Falla's *Amor Brujo* as given by La Argentina; and it is because there are traces of the post-Diaghilev style also in *The Three-Cornered Hat* that it holds even the most listless " rover " enthralled whenever it is performed.

Massine's own performance " sealed his reputation as a dancer of the first order. He broke entirely new ground and proved himself complete master of it. During his stay in Seville he had set himself to acquire with infinite patience and observation all the nuances of technique and temperament that make Andalucian dancing the despair of those who are not born Spaniards." [2] His place in recent performances has been admirably filled by Woizikovsky, while Madame Karsavina, with " all her irresistible grace and intelligence," has been worthily succeeded by Madame Tschernicheva.

It is not easy to forget the " flickering beauty of the scene," the capes of the policemen or the dress of the villagers. In the music, however, recent performances in London have shown a tendency to tone down its deliberate asperities, and to make it sound " all treble and bass."

The ballet is founded on a capital short story by Alarcón, already used by Hugo Wolf for his opera *Der Corregidor*. It has been translated several times into English — the latest version is the excellent one by Martin Armstrong. The story in its turn is founded on a late Spanish ballad, which again is said (like many popular ballads) to be founded on fact. The miller, an ugly, astute, but humorous and good-hearted Southerner, has married a "fine woman" from the north. They are childless, but very much attached to one another, and their mill, situated some little way out of the town — which, in actual fact,

is said to have been Guadix, to the east of Granada
— was a favourite walk for the local notabilities,
including the Bishop and the canons of the cathedral,
and also for the resident magistrate, the *Corregidor*.
As sometimes happens, it is the officer of the law who
is most tempted to break the law and even to use
the machinery of the law to accomplish his lawless
designs. On the day on which the miller is to offer
the " first-fruits " of his grapes to the Bishop, the
Corregidor arrives two hours before he is expected,
hoping to find the miller's wife alone during the
hours of the siesta. Disappointed in his purpose, he de-
termines to have the miller called away by the police
on some pretext or other and detained while he can
press his suit on the miller's wife. The miller is duly
called away, and the *Corregidor* finds the miller's
wife alone in the mill, according to plan. Unfortunately, he falls into the mill-race; and on seeing, and
recognizing, the dripping apparition, the miller's
wife mounts her donkey and rides away in the night
to the village in which the miller has been detained.
The miller, however, has escaped and actually passes
his wife, as she is riding away to him, without
recognizing her. He reaches the mill to find the doors
open and the well-known clothes, walking-stick, and
three-cornered hat of the *Corregidor* lying all over
the best parlour and drying in front of a big fire.
Up in the bedroom he sees the *Corregidor* in his own
bed. This is too much, even for an easy-going man

not given to jealousy; in his "despairing, cursing rage" his eye falls on the *Corregidor's* clothes, and an idea comes to him. The wife of the *Corregidor* is still a beautiful woman, *encore désirable*; he will dress in the *Corregidor's* clothes and pay a visit to the Residency.

At the Residency they all meet once more: the *Corregidor* speechless with rage — and also with jealousy — in the miller's clothes; the miller, complacent, somewhat subdued, but proud of his "revenge," in the *Corregidor's* clothes; the miller's wife, an injured goddess, not knowing or realizing what has happened; and the wife of the *Corregidor*, a great lady, who knows the whole story of each of the characters and dominates the scene until the very end. So the *Corregidor* is humbled and the miller and the miller's wife reassured as to one another, and they all live happily ever after — until the storms of 1808.

It is easy to criticize the way in which this story has been turned into a ballet, but hardly safe to do so in ignorance of the conditions in which the arrangement was first made. For it was not originally intended for M. Diaghilev at all; but was planned as a pantomime in two acts and arranged for performance in Madrid, under the name of *El Corregidor y la Molinera*, by G. Martínez Sierra. That is to say, the story was already familiar to the greater part of the audience; and the authors had not to tell it over again (as Hugo Wolf had done), but to remind the

spectators of the salient points. So the Bishop, his
chaplain, and the reverend canons have all gone, and
after a few scenes designed to exhibit the characters
of the miller and his wife we are plunged almost
straight into the nocturnal visit of the *Corregidor*.

Picasso's decorations, and the admirable dancing
of Massine and the others, have often been described;
here we shall refer only to the music. It would not be
true to say that there are leitmotives; but two themes
of constant recurrence are (1) a phrase from the
jota of Navarre

which must evidently be connected with the miller's
wife, who also came from Navarre, and (2) the beginning of the accompaniment of the well-known
Murcian song *El paño moruno,* the first of Falla's
Seven Spanish Songs, which is associated with the
miller.

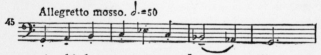

A third tune, grotesquely announced on the
bassoon, obviously typifies the *Corregidor*:

while, among other snatches of melody which occur near the beginning and are heard several times in the course of the work, are a tune whistled by the miller:

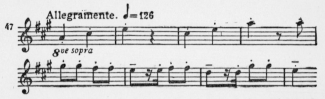

the procession of the *Corregidor* and his *alguacils* (constables)

which, afterwards, generally occurs in semiquavers; and a vulgar little tune, first heard as one of the *alguacils* suddenly appears and regards the miller and his wife with a malicious grin.

A passage which occurs more than once suggests the guitar prelude of *granadinas:*

while, eminently characteristic of Falla, and looking forward to *The Puppet-Show*, is the movement which is being played when the curtain first goes up and is repeated on more than one occasion during the first part:

Another characteristic and charming effect is the music to which the miller's wife offers — or pretends to offer — the *Corregidor* the first-fruits of the grapes, always keeping them just out of his reach until he slips and falls flat on his back:

while the rhythms of vain pursuit are delightfully expressed when the *Corregidor* pursues the miller's wife, all wet as he is after falling in the mill-race.

The two main set dances are the *fandango* danced by the miller's wife, in the first part:

and the miller's *farruca* in the second:

a completely "abstract" piece of dancing, which holds the audience in tense excitement from the first beat to the last.

It is useful to remember these themes during a performance, since many of them come back in slightly altered forms and are heard two or even three at a time in the course of the final *jota,* which is besides an orgy of conflicting rhythms.

There is a delightfully Voltairian feeling about the whole ballet; and, considering only the music, it exhibits Falla's characteristics in the clearest possible way. There are "the short, unsentimental snatches of melody, clear in design and precise in expression, with sinuous outlines and ingratiating movements . . . the exquisite sense of harmony, not greatly varied perhaps, but always attractive; and in this, too, clearness is one of his greatest gifts. His harmonies also are strictly tonal, although often adorned with iridescent appoggiaturas. . . . And, lastly, there is his sense of rhythm, which is perhaps the most interesting aspect of his art. It is extraordinarily restless and vivacious; a continual pulsation which never languishes." [3] The ballet in its finally revised form might be regarded as Falla's contribution to the music of the Armistice. In that case it is the one really worthy piece of music which that historic event produced.

[3] M. Castelnuovo-Tedesco, loc. cit.

CHAPTER IX

THE PUPPET-SHOW

Somewhere in 1919 or 1920 Falla was invited by the Princesse de Polignac to compose an opera for her puppet-theatre. By the autumn of 1920 he was full of the subject and spent some months at Granada working at it daily throughout the long mornings, remaining invisible from the time of early coffee until a late lunch, long after two. The afternoons were spent in house-hunting; for he had decided to abandon Madrid and live permanently in Granada, and house-hunting in such a place is something of an experience, especially to a visitor from northern Europe. On other days our walks would be taken with the painter Bacarizas, to find the perfect scene for *El Amor Brujo,* and the scene was discovered eventually in a large white cave on the Sacro Monte, clean as a new pin under its perpetually renewed coats of whitewash and hung with a large quantity of shining copper pans. From the entrance could be seen the towers of the Alhambra and the terraced gardens of the Generalife. The evenings were often spent in listening to Angel Barrios playing Andaluz music on the guitar, as has already been described in an earlier chapter.

Work on the *Retablo* was interrupted by the return to Madrid and in the next spring by concert-tours. There was the visit to London in 1921, during which Falla played the solo part in his *Nights in the Gardens of Spain*, at one of those ambitious concerts at which Mr. Edward Clark brought to London and performed all the most recent music of western Europe. Then came the definite move to Granada, the joy of taking possession of the so much desired *carmen*, the disillusionment and subsequent change to another, with a better garden, a better view, more water, and everything that could be wished . . . except for the French *señorita* in a neighbouring *carmen*, who in the hot summer months would insist in playing loudly on the piano with the window open! Then in 1922 came the festival and competition of *cante hondo*, with a varied succession of sequels, somewhat disturbing to a composer full of a masterpiece and knowing that he will have to finish it against time. Finally the *Retablo* was performed at Seville for the first time (in a concert version) just before Holy Week, on the 23rd March 1923; and afterwards given in Paris with all the exquisite beauty and splendour of the Princesse de Polignac's puppets, on the 25th June.

Rumours of the opera had reached London even before it had been performed in Paris, and Mr. Napier Miles jumped at it for the operatic festival, " a week of one-act operas," which he was organizing at Bristol for the following year. Five performances were given in English, and the work was repeated on the last night by special request.

The production at Bristol, rough and ready though in many ways it was, was an event of great interest in the history of opera in England. Don Quixote had returned to the English stage. It was in England, it seems, that the " Ingenious Gentleman " made his first appearance on any stage; for *The Knight of the Burning Pestle* (c. 1610) is obviously influenced by the story. A masque by James Shirley, *The Triumph of Peace* (1634–5), contains the following:

> *The* Antimasquers *were ushered by a horn-pipe, and a shawm; riding in coats and caps of yellow taffeta, spotted with silver, their feathers red.* . . .
>
> FANCY *in a suit of several-coloured feathers, hooded, a pair of bat's wings on his shoulders.* . . .
>
> *After him rode* OPINION *and* CONFIDENCE *together.* . . .
>
> *Next rode* JOLLITY *and* LAUGHTER. . . .
>
> *Then followed variety of antic music.*[1] . . .
>
> *Here variety of other antic music, counterfeiting the voices of birds.* . . .
>
> *After these a* Windmill, *against which a*

---

[1] The music was by William Lawes and Simon Ives, " whose art gave an harmonious soul to the otherwise languishing numbers."

fantastic Knight *with his lance, and his* squire *armed, seemed to make their attempts.*

It was in England too, apparently, that Don Quixote first appeared in opera — or in an opera after the Restoration English model — *The Comical History of Don Quixote* (1694), the music to which was by Henry Purcell. But Purcell lived at a time in which the nobility and idealism of Don Quixote had been forgotten, and most people imagined the story to be merely facetious. Thomas Durfey, the author of the "book," made *The Comical History of Don Quixote* into a "review"; and it is only remembered now for the noble music which Purcell wrote for one scene, "From Rosy Bowers."

Professor Fitzmaurice Kelly, who knew more about *Don Quixote* than anyone in England, used to say that the essence of Cervantes's humor lay in its unsmiling gravity. Nothing at any rate is more foreign to the author of *Don Quixote* than facetiousness; and this fact was instinctively grasped by his earliest translator — an Englishman — who, as a contemporary both of Cervantes and of Shakspere, was able to turn the best Spanish of his day into the best English and to do it naturally, as a man who translates a new foreign book into the language he habitually uses.

The sense of grave humour and the sense of the force and beauty of language are two of the qualities

which make Falla's opera the very notable work it is.
As a Spaniard, Falla is a man who is passionately
serious and yet, at the same time, one who has a sense
of humour which is quite irrepressible. He is also distinguished among all other Spanish composers for his
sense of musical declamation, by the way he sets
words to music. He seems to explore the rhythms
and cadences of the Spanish language with the same
feeling of excitement with which Purcell explored
English in *Dido and Æneas, King Arthur,* and *The
Fairy Queen;* and he has set to music the glorious
prose of Cervantes with the same sense of discovery
that Purcell must have felt in setting words from the
Authorized Version of the Bible — a book which was
first published in the same year in which Thomas
Shelton published his English version of the First
Part of *Don Quixote:* 1611.

The adventure of Don Quixote which forms the
subject of Falla's opera is taken from the Second
Part. Don Quixote and Sancho Panza, his squire, are
on the road once more in search of knightly adventures, righting wrongs, succouring the oppressed,
and delivering distressed damsels out of captivity.
They are resting at an inn, when a travelling showman appears with a puppet-theatre, and the innkeeper, who knows him well, immediately invites
him to give a performance in the stable. The play
which the puppets perform is the story of Don
Gaiferos and the peerless Melisendra, an old Spanish

ballad of how a Christian princess was delivered from captivity among the Moors in Spain by a Knight of the court of Charlemagne. The showman is inside his little theatre, like the man in a Punch-and-Judy show; the course of the story is explained by his boy, who comes in front of the show before every scene and explains what is going to happen and who the puppets are supposed to be. Then the curtain of the puppet-show goes up, the band plays, and the puppets go through the scene which the boy has described.

Don Quixote, Sancho Panza, the innkeeper, and others sit in the stable watching. It will be remembered that Don Quixote is by no means a madman.[2] He is only out of his mind on one subject — that of knight-errantry; on all others he is perfectly sane and is, in fact, a scholarly if somewhat irascible country gentleman who spends his days out of doors and his nights in his library. The showman's boy gabbles off the beginning of the story in a manner which is something between plain-song and a street cry; he pours out the words as if they had no meaning and often puts the emphasis in the wrong place. At first he is entirely unsupported by the orchestra, but gradually as he gets more excited and carried away by the story and puts more colour into what he is saying, the

___

[2] See *El Pensamiento de Cervantes (The Mind of Cervantes)* by Américo Castro (Madrid, 1926), or the present writer's chapter on Don Quixote in *Spain from the South* (1928).

instruments steal in one after the other, until at last
he is singing at the top of his voice, with the whole
band playing away beneath him. First he points out
Don Gaiferos playing at chess and being reprimanded
by Charlemagne for wasting his time in Paris, instead
of setting out like a knight-errant to deliver his lady.
Then we see Melisendra on her tower, and a Moor
who insults her is soundly beaten by order of the
Moorish King. Don Quixote listens with the greatest
attention, occasionally interrupting the boy on a
point of scholarship, as, for instance, when the Moor
is seen "stealing fair and softly on Melisendra" to
give her a kiss, and the Moorish King orders him to
be whipped forthwith, and the boy explains that
"with the Moors there is neither inquisition nor legal
proceeding, such as is our custom."

"Child," says Don Quixote, "that's nonsense!
For to weigh the evidence and find the truth there
always must be a legal inquisition."

Master Peter puts his head out from under the
puppet-show. "I told you!" he cries. "Do not add
your decorations, but obey this good gentleman's
instructions. Sing you your proper plain-song, and
do not meddle with the other voices: too much
counterpoint ruins the lute-strings."

"Yes, sir, I will," the boy replies, and the show
goes on.

The next interruption comes not from Don
Quixote, but from Master Peter himself, wishing to

show, no doubt, that the knight is not the only man of taste present. After Don Gaiferos has come riding down through the Pyrenees and delivered Melisendra from her tower in Saragossa, the boy (now thoroughly interested in the story and carried away by the good fortune of the lovers) breaks into a passionate lyrical outburst to the sound of the galloping of the horse. "Go in peace," he sings, "O matchless pair, truest among all true lovers. May good fortune thus prosper your marvellous adventure, and kindred and friends all see how you shall enjoy now all the rest of your lifetime, as long as once old Nestor . . ."

Master Peter's head appears from under the puppet-show. "My good boy, be plainer! No embroidery! For all such affectation is scurvy."

The escape of Melisendra has been discovered. The alarm is sounded and (as the boy puts it) "the city seems to shake with all the noise of church bells ringing, that sound from the mosques and the minarets above them."

Don Quixote springs from his seat. Such ignorance is unpardonable. "There you are out," he cries, "and your bells most improper; for among Moors is no ringing of bells, but beating of drums and squealing hautboys."

The showman protests once more. "Sir," he says, "pray stand you not so strictly upon trifles, or we shall never please you! Have you never seen, sir, comedies and tragedies presented, full of absurdities and follies? Yet in spite of that they follow their career with success and admiration, and even are heard with delight and applause."

"Yes, that is the truth," replies Don Quixote.

He settles down once more and listens quietly, until a host of Muslim horsemen ride out in pursuit of the Christian lovers. This is too much for Don Quixote's imagination. For him the puppet-play has suddenly become the real world. His madness returns to him and is indeed thoroughly aroused. He leaps up, sword in hand, and attacks the puppets, which for him have become real Moors, and not " shapes made of cardboard."

"Stop, you scoundrels! " he cries. " Misbegotten abortions! *Malnacida canalla!* Dare not to follow nor try to catch them; for if you do, you first must fight with me! "

Then (as the Jacobean translator puts it) " with an unseen and posting fury he began to rain strokes upon the puppetish Moorism, overthrowing some and beheading others, maiming this and cutting in pieces that; and amongst many other blows he fetched one so downright, that had not Master Peter tumbled and squatted down, he had clipped his mazard as easily as if it had been made of marchpane."

Don Quixote does not stop until the puppets are all " cut to fitters " and the showman's business ruined. "What," he cries, "had I not been present at this moment, what would have become of Gaiferos, or what of the peerless Melisendra! Oh would I might have all those here this instant, to answer straight before me, if any there be who know not what gain to the world are knights-errant! Most happy times and fortunate ages were those, that saw the deeds and daring of the bold Amadis, the giant strength of Felixmarte of Hircania, with that most valiant Tirante, the white Knight, and the invincible Belianis the Grecian; with all the mighty company of the numberless knights-errant, who by their reckless challenges, their loves, and their encounters, have writ in the Book of Fame their glory! "

(" Santa Maria! " the showman mutters; " Lord, he's a madman! ")

" And when all is said," Don Quixote continues, " long live knighthood, and long live the name of knight-errant, above all the professions that are in all the wide world! "

The musical opportunities of such a story are obvious. Falla, truer than any living Spanish composer to a very Spanish quality — that of austerity — has set it for only three singers and a band of twenty-three performers, among whom there are as many wind-players as strings, while a harpsichord is included, not as an accompaniment, but as an orchestral instrument. His music has very little about it that to an English or American ear, accustomed to the pianoforte music of Granados and Albéniz — and of Falla himself — will sound superficially Spanish. In reality, however, it is intensely Spanish in feeling, mainly owing to the vigour of the rhythms and the fact of those strongly conflicting rhythms being piled upon one another.

Falla has sometimes been dismissed as a " folk-lore musician." Even the latest Paris criticism of his work repeats the old assertion. Yet it is an assertion which will not bear examination. In *La Vida Breve*, Spanish as it sounds, there is not a single folk-tune from beginning to end. In *The Three-Cornered Hat* the quotations are few and deliberate and put there for a humorous purpose. *El Amor Brujo* has nothing of folk-lore except certain rhythmic effects in the fire-dance. In the *Retablo* there are not more than two occasions on which a genuine Spanish tune has been used. One is near the end, when Don Quixote is slashing the puppets to pieces; it suggests a Catalan dance heard in the hills near Barcelona. Another is the curious singsong effect for Melisendra on her tower; and the rhythm, hesitating between two and three beats in a bar, is one which is derived from the kind of tune sung by old Spanish ballad-singers at the time that the story of *Don Quixote* was written, and preserved for us in the sixteenth-century lute-books or the *Seven Books of Music* of Francisco de Salinas.

The musical material of *The Puppet-Show* is an extraordinarily skilful piece of writing for a small orchestra of about twenty-three players. Under no circumstances should the number of strings be increased so as to overbalance the wind. It is scored for flute (and piccolo), two oboes, English horn, clarinet, bassoon, two horns, trumpet, two drums, side-drum, tambourine (without jingles), xylophone, two rattles, tamtam, harpsichord, harp, three of four first violins, two or three second violins, two violas, two 'cellos, double-bass.

The orchestration shows something of the quality which has already been described as characteristic of the work of Cervantes: an apparent simplicity or lack of sophistication — an impression almost that the effects are obtained in the most obvious way — though in reality they conceal a subtlety of thought and a sense of poetry which only intimate knowledge and long familiarity with the work can reveal.

An example is the composer's use of muted instruments. What more obvious, it might be said, than a muted trumpet — that is, a toy trumpet — to accompany a puppet, a doll? A muted trumpet certainly sounds like a puppet trumpet; it sounds in this way in the overture, "Master Peter's Symphony," in a different key from the rest of the band, the more unexpectedly since "Master Peter's Symphony" might almost be called a movement from a trumpet concerto in C major. The muted trumpet comes as a reminder that the opera we are about to witness is not altogether a real opera, but a puppet-opera. Yet there is nothing very original about that; the idea might have occurred to any composer, and any composer could have done it.

What would not have occurred to any composer, however, is that at the same time there is a connexion between muted instruments and the other world — not the world of " jazz," of which Falla is entirely innocent, but the world of story and romance, where Don Quixote is always riding slowly along the endless, dusty roads of La Mancha, and where Don Gaiferos — equally, but (to us) more dimly — is always trotting down from the Pyrenees to deliver Melisendra from her captivity in Saragossa, and carry her away, mounted on the pillion behind him.

Muted instruments are the ghosts of ordinary instruments. They have reached the stage of toys, stories, ballads, and fairy-tales; and belong to that other world, which exists parallel, as it were, with the world we live in. . . .

"The horns of Elfland," of course; what could be more obvious for a muted horn! A mind like that of Falla, or Cervantes, does not work in so obvious a fashion. Don Gaiferos and the peerless Melisendra are, of course, mere puppets, "shapes made of cardboard"; and that is all that Master Peter will ever see in them. But the puppet-shapes are only the symbols of what they really are; that is, inhabitants of the world of story and romance, of Fairyland; to be heard rather than seen, as they were by Tam Lin's betrothed in the ballad, when

> About the dead hour o' the night
> She heard the bridles ring,

and yet saw nothing. Or later when

> Out then spak' the Queen o' Fairies,
> And an angry woman was she.

For these ghostly shapes — clear and definite and objective to the penetrating, concrete imagination of the Spaniard, shapes which are at one and the same time both ghosts and puppets, creatures of fantasy and visible, tangible shapes — for such, muted instruments are exactly the right form of musical expression; toy instruments playing in a fairy-tale.

Not only a toy world or a puppet world is presented to us; there is also a fairy world, in which the actors are all dolls. And Don Quixote, who cannot merely sit there and "hear the bridles ring," must from his very nature mingle in the fray and bring everything — the puppet-theatre and the whole fairy world — crashing to the ground.

Toy instruments playing in a fairy-tale; muted trumpets and horns, not made to sound like toy instruments, but made to give a sense of poetry, remoteness, and distance — a distance not to be measured only in leagues or centuries, but in another dimension as well. That is Falla's discovery; let us see how he employs it.

The muted trumpet in the overture is frankly

a toy trumpet, blown naughtily in D flat while the rest of the band are playing in C. But in the fanfare which follows,

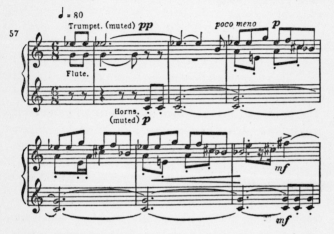

we can already distinguish the real instruments from the fairy instruments; the muted trumpets above the flute, and the stopped horns below, seem to stand apart and to invite us irresistibly to follow them out into the fairy world. Soon, without knowing it, we find ourselves transported thither.

The boy appears, and when the curtain of the puppet-theatre goes up, we actually see the hall of Charlemagne, with Roland and Gaiferos playing at chess as he has described it to us. The muted trumpet and flute are supported by real horns; and the trumpet is only unmuted after the boy's description of Charlemagne himself (No. 18 in the score), just as we are about to see the Emperor in person, and have ourselves become so much part of the puppet world that it is as real as our own.

"But now [says the boy] all eyes turn yonder, where now appears the Castle of Saragossa; and the lady you see there on the tower — *that* is the fair Melisendra. . . ." The trumpet is muted once more. We are transported into a world still more remote and incredible; the World's Desire is before our eyes: fair Melisendra sits in her tower, with a coal-black eunuch to keep guard over her.

The puppet-play proceeds according to the boy's explanation. Presently Don Quixote interrupts him on a trivial point.

straight line; give us the text, and no notes or other refinements

The trumpet is muted, but the horns are not.

The beating of the presumptuous Moor who has insulted Melisendra seems to the audience real enough; there is no need for muted instruments there.

We hear the muted horn again for a moment when the boy takes up his parable once more: "This knight you see, is Don Gaiferos, appearing gaily on horseback, and posting in haste to reach Saragossa." But when we "hear a horseman ride over the hill" and actually see Don Gaiferos coming down through the passes of the Pyrenees, the horn is a real horn, though the trumpet is still muted, as much as to say that it is still, after all, a distant fancy.

"And here," the boy begins again, "and here you shall witness how that most fair Melisendra, who now hath been so well revenged on that enamoured Moor for his great boldness, doth show herself from a window of the castle."

Once more it is all real, both to the audience on the stage and to us in the theatre—one of the most beautiful and moving moments in the opera: two horns and trumpet, over a repeated note, *pizzicato* on the double-bass, with a lovely romantic burst of melody in the middle.

In the scene in which we see Melisendra "leap from her bay-window, straight into the arms of Don Gaiferos," who is also accompanied by a fine piece of music, a real horn is imaginatively used at the reprise when Gaiferos " at one hoist hath set her astride on his horse's crupper."

For the bell-effects, when the boy (to Don Quixote's annoyance) describes bells as ringing from the minarets of mosques — and for the confusion caused by Don Quixote's attack on the puppets and demolition of the puppet-show — the orchestration is too complicated for quotation and the reader must be referred to the miniature full-score.

One more example of the psychological processes at work in the composer's mind may be taken from the passage in which, "the general ruin of the motion performed," Don Quixote, "somewhat appeased," addresses the spectators in explanation of his conduct.

64

The raucous passage for oboe and clarinet in unison has already been associated with his onslaught; the somewhat academic bars that follow seem to express his desire to instruct his hearers in the reason for his action, interrupted at the mention of the word "knight" and the thought of knight-errantry,

65

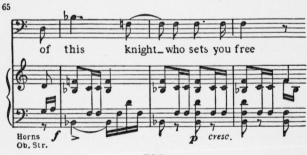

and resumed when he declares to them his own name,
which is heralded by two trumpet calls:

66

backed by a little academic instruction and completed
by a fanfare at the great name of Don Quixote. He
is convinced that it is all real, and the instruments
help both audiences to believe it. And yet, in his
magnificent peroration, a faint doubt creeps upon us,
and the trumpet call is presented for the last time on
an unreal, muted trumpet.

133

CHAPTER X

THE PUPPET-SHOW (*continued*)

The Puppet-Show is a work which taxes the intelligence of both producer and audience. Some people believe that Don Quixote is too simple a character for these hectic, sophisticated times in which we live; but that is a view which proves nothing but lack of perception on the part of those who hold it. For the figure of Don Quixote as created by Cervantes, so far from being naïve, obvious, or childish, is if anything too subtle to be grasped immediately by a hasty, modern audience. "Cervantes," it has been said, "was a humorist; that is, he could think of more than one thing at a time; many commentators are without this faculty." Falla knew what modern audiences were like and, above all, what a modern Parisian audience was like, and he covered the apparent lack of sophistication of Cervantes's story with a new and obvious piece of sophistication: that of making the whole play entirely an affair of puppets, a thoroughly sophisticated entertainment for a thoroughly sophisticated audience.

The composer intended it for a sumptuously fitted marionette-theatre in a drawing-room — the drawing-room of the Princesse de Polignac. The puppets are of two sizes. The larger represent the real persons in the drama: Don Quixote, Master Peter, and his boy, with Sancho Panza, the innkeeper, and the rest as characters who do not sing; the smaller figures are the puppets in Master Peter's "motion." The producer's difficulties are mainly due to the great weight of the larger puppets, the complication of their movements, and the difficulty of synchronizing the action of both kinds of puppets with the music. The spectator's difficulty is to be quite clear in his own mind that he is witnessing not merely a play within a play, but a puppet-play within a puppet-play — one puppet-play within another. A puppet Don Quixote watches the performance of a puppet-show worked by a puppet Master Peter; and the principal object on the stage of the puppet-theatre is another, smaller puppet-theatre. To the audience specially invited to a Parisian drawing-room, or an audience gathered from all parts of the world for an international festival of contemporary music at Zürich, a play about puppets performed by other puppets may not have offered great difficulties in comprehension. It was different, however, when the work came to be performed on a public stage.

The first public attempt was made at the Bristol Operatic Festival in 1924, when the work was barely printed, and the publisher with commendable promptitude rushed the edition through so that it might be used by the performers. The producer, Mr. W. Johnstone-Douglas, started from a note of the composer's printed in the score that " The puppets representing real persons may be replaced by living actors; but in that case they should wear masks." This solution did away at once with the " puppet-play within a puppet-play "; but loss in subtlety was amply compensated for by gain in clearness, and the performances by the Bristol company (which consisted for the most part of well-known London singers) have been so far the only ones in which the audience has had no doubt as to what Falla's opera is intended to represent. Mr. Johnstone-Douglas, as a practical producer with strictly limited resources, was obliged to introduce other modifications. Since the puppets had to be specially made, naturalistic puppets " in the round," like those of the Princesse de Polignac, were out of the question. A puppet-maker in London was indeed approached, but he estimated the cost at three hundred pounds, and the time required at six months. The Bristol producer therefore, at the suggestion of his designer, Miss Rachel Russell, adopted the system of flat puppets in two dimensions, painted in bright colours on thin pieces of wood, like those traditionally used in the puppet-theatres of Palermo. They were worked from above, but by invisible hands (at a subsequent performance in New York the puppet-workers seem to have been visible), and their action was reduced to the most simple movements possible so that they should synchronize with the music and at the same time be obvious enough to be clearly visible to the audience. Eventually the masks for the " real persons " were also abandoned. No singer can do himself justice in a mask, and it should be possible to make up any actor as a convincing Don Quixote. The make-up was perhaps the least satisfactory part of the Bristol performances, and unnecessary attention was called to it by a press-photographer who, during a rehearsal, made pictures of the principals with no make-up on their faces at all.

These performances, as a whole, enchanted the audiences who gathered there from London, the west of England, and the midlands; while the intelligent and enthusiastic accounts which appeared in the press, both of England and of America, did more for the reputation of the opera than any number of private performances in Paris. The performers in the Bristol production should be mentioned: Don Quixote, Mr. Arthur Cranmer; Master Peter, Mr. A. T. Goody; the boy, Miss Muriel Tannahill, a gifted American singer who cheerfully accepted the adventure of a part in which every principle of good singing had necessarily to be violated and the part sustained by sheer intelligence and good musicianship. The conductors were Dr. Adrian Boult and Dr. Malcolm Sargent. The opera was sung in English, and the singers had the great advantage of being able to sing words which had mostly been taken from the Elizabethan, or Jacobean, translation of Thomas Shelton, begun in the lifetime of Cervantes, and finished in 1620, only four years after his death. There have been admirable performances in New York, and the work has also been given in Barcelona, Amsterdam, and Berlin. At Zürich it was the outstanding success of the Festival of the International Society for Contemporary Music in 1926; although the performance did not please the composer, who considered both the puppets and the *tempi* far too " Germanic."

In the spring of 1928 *The Puppet-Show* was put on at the Opéra Comique in Paris. The producer on this occasion was confronted with the same problem as that which had confronted the producer at Bristol in 1924: how to make the work intelligible to a large audience. He had the advantage of expert Spanish advice, the greatest living Spanish painter, Don Ignacio Zuloaga, to design the scenery, and the presence, at all the rehearsals, of the composer himself. Zuloaga attacked the problem of adapting a puppet-opera intended for a drawing-room to the vast stage of the Opéra Comique with characteristic Spanish determination. The composer was anxious that the theory of the " puppet-play within a puppet-play " should not be abandoned, and it was necessary therefore to create the illusion that the whole of the Opéra Comique stage was nothing but a *théâtre guignol.* Zuloaga had an idea which would have occurred to no one but a Spaniard, and moreover to one who knew his country through and through. The "real" persons — Don Quixote, Sancho, Master Peter, and the innkeeper — were to be like the giants and *cabezudos* ("big heads") which appear in some of the processions for Corpus Christi; and he modelled for them, out of light cardboard and paper, enormous masks reaching down to the waist. Bristol had not quite realized that, in Spain, Don Quixote and Sancho Panza are characters whose appearance is as definitely and unchangeably fixed in the public imagination as are the figures of Mr. Pickwick and Sam Weller, Mr. Jorrocks and James Pigg, Sherlock Holmes and Dr. Watson. In Germany and central and eastern Europe generally, at present the source of all the newest and most original ideas in the theatre, a designer would probably have built on the popular conception of a well-known character by producing something in complete contrast to it, like the bald and beardless Don Quixote at Zürich. Western Europe, however, has not yet reached that stage; and Paris as the "Defence of the West," the fount and origin of all "Latin" traditions, required a naturalistic Don Quixote, who should be immediately recognizable. Such a Don Quixote Zuloaga gave it. The mask was a noble conception and a fine piece of modelling, with the barber's basin-helmet and the tattered armour tied together with pieces of string; while Sancho Panza was no less unmistakable and convincing.

The composer has laid it down in the score that

ERRATA AND CORRIGENDA.

Page 24, line 5: for *produces* read *reveals*.

Page 29, last line but one: delete bracket.

Page 32, last line: for *had gone down* read *lost his life*.

Page 36, lines 18 and 19: for *is* read *was*.

Page 76, line 7: for *climaxes* read *cadences*.

Page 102, line 19: for *now when the* read *after the old*.

Page 103, line 22: for *has now* read *at last*.

Page 113, lines 1–3: read *Sometime in 1919 or 1920 Falla suggested to the Princess de Polignac the plan of an opera for her puppet-theatre.*

Page 130: music, the right hand part in the second stave should begin with a treble clef.

Page 151, line 15: for *becomes* read *become*.

Page 157, line 19: for *Corps* read *Corpus*.

Page 164, line 26: for *mere* read *clever*.

ERRATA AND CORRIGENDA

the figure of Don Quixote shall be much taller than any of the others. This was achieved at the Opéra Comique by making him walk on a long, low bench, stretching from the wings, on the spectator's left, across to the puppet-theatre, on the other side of the stage. To hide this long bench from view a group of what were apparently waxwork figures had been designed, spectators of the show — those way-farers whom Cervantes describes as being present in the inn on the night on which Master Peter played before Don Quixote. They were not so successful as the masks. They were badly lighted, and their im-mobility during the performance became gradually more and more disconcerting, especially when it was noticed that one figure, whose head was turned away from the puppet-show, deigned to look neither at what the puppets did nor at what Don Quixote did to the puppets.

The scene was laid in the courtyard of an old Spanish inn, such as the famous Mesón del Sevillano, described by Cervantes and still to be seen at Toledo, while the puppet-theatre itself was conceived as one of the most natural objects to be seen in the court-yard of an old Spanish inn: a two-wheeled, covered cart. This was another brilliant stroke of genius on the part of Zuloaga. In all the illustrations to *Don Quixote*, from the earliest anonymous Flemish illus-trator through Copyel in the eighteenth century to Doré in the nineteenth and Brangwyn at the beginning of the twentieth, the puppet-theatre had always been shown as something which must have been unpacked from a cart and put together in a yard.

We read that Master Peter brought his " motion " and his monkey "in a small carriage *(en una carreta),*" and that the innkeeper "pointed him to a place where he might set it up, which was done in an instant." Zuloaga's solution of the problem was equally in accordance with the text. He had thought of the cart and the "motion" as being all in one. It was arranged with one wheel facing the audience. Its "proscenium opening" was formed by drawing back curtains in one side of the hood, while the stage was a shelf some eight feet long by two feet deep, running all along one side of the cart, and inside it. The puppets were planned on the same principle as at Bristol — that is to say, they were flat — but they were worked, not from above, but from below, and ran in parallel grooves cut in the stage of the puppet-theatre, being moved by prolongations of their legs (or stands), held by puppet-workers sitting underneath, at the bottom of the " cart " and invisible to the audience. This, as it turned out, gave Bristol an advantage. The movements in Paris, though steady, were too slow, and did not seem to be the immediate consequences of the music, as they should have been. The horse on which Don Gaiferos came riding down from the Pyrenees to deliver Melisendra from her captivity in Saragossa moved as steadily as a Spanish train; though to Don Quixote it seemed (as he said afterwards) to fly rather than run, so that by the time the adventure was over, Melisendra must have been " wantonly solacing with her husband in France." The French Don Gaiferos, like a Norman knight and a true militarist, had an immense sword, with which he gravely saluted his lady; the English Gaiferos, more Saxon and less warlike, carried a horn, which he raised to his lips and blew softly whenever a horn sounded in the orchestra. Both Paris and Bristol had puppets of various sizes for the horse and rider, to show that they were nearer every time they appeared; so large, indeed, did they become, so much had they grown when they passed beneath Melisendra's tower, that at the first Bristol performance, a voice at the back of the audience was distinctly heard to mention the name of a well-known food for infants and invalids — which showed, at any rate, that the owner of that particular voice was following the play with interest and not concerned with the question of puppets within puppets. The French puppets had also the disadvantage that they could not turn round and leave the stage, as they could at Bristol, but had to go off backwards. This gave no opportunity to the puppet of Charlemagne, " who turns his back despising Don Gaiferos," and showed at Bristol when he turned round that he had two faces, one angrier than the other.

The Paris production of the *Retablo* was an extremely good show, and the Bristol one, when all is said and done, a rather provincial entertainment. Yet in spite of all that composer and designer could do, in spite also of the friendliest co-operation of all concerned, from the director of the Opéra Comique down to the most junior stage-hand, who worked with untiring devotion and good temper to make *The Puppet-Show* a success, the opera puzzled the Paris critics and was clearly unintelligible to the greater part of the audience. To the difficulty of grasping music which is frankly though not aggressively modern in idiom and utterly unlike what Spanish music is commonly supposed to be, there was added the difficulty of realizing that the whole setting was intended to be *guignol* and of accepting the convention that not only the actual puppet-theatre in the cart, but also the whole of the stage of the Opéra Comique was meant to be an immense puppet-theatre. Then there were the masks worn by the actors. They were impressive and easily recognizable by those in the audience who knew their *Don Quixote;* but Don Quixote's movements were seldom quick enough, and the fact that he had always to " steer that noble frame " gingerly along a narrow raised platform impeded his movements still further. At the *répétition générale* the singers who represented Don Quixote and Master Peter had sung from their masks, which had large openings in the neck made for the purpose. But even such experienced singers as MM. Dufranne and Salignac (who had often sung the work in concert performances) seemed to find it impossible to do themselves or the composer justice, and at the first public performance they sang from the orchestra, leaving their masks to be worn by supers. This, as it happened, was a still more unfortunate arrangement. To the difficulty an audience has in connecting a man wearing a mask on the stage, with a voice which rises from an invisible singer in the orchestra, were added the difficulties of the wearers of the masks entering and moving at exactly the right moment, to say nothing of the difficulty of the singers finding their notes, with noise of the orchestra going on all round them. The result at the earlier performances at the Opéra Comique was chaos. " Leads " missed by a visible singer on the stage are disconcerting enough, but a lead missed by a disembodied voice, supposed to issue from the mouth of a man in a mask, is baffling to the last degree. Neither Don Quixote's interruptions nor the exclamations of Master Peter made their effect, and both these singers and the boy (who sang on the stage from a short flight of steps leading up into the cart at one end) seemed to find their positions too uncomfortable to be able to sing either in time or in tune. This was assuredly remedied afterwards; but, at first, it was no wonder that the opera failed to make its effect in Paris. Another reason for this lay in the language. Falla's declamation is contrary

to the genius of French, as was freely remarked in
the corridors of the Opéra Comique after the first
performance there, and the French words were inaudible and never got through to the audience. But
it is not contrary to the genius of English. Again
and again Shelton's words exactly fit the musical
phrase, and make their point unerringly; while the
somewhat Italian manner of Don Quixote's music
(and Don Quixote, it will be remembered, had read all
the best Italian poets of his time) is grasped without
difficulty by a singer — and an audience — trained on
Purcell and Handel.

The truth is that the problem of presenting the
Retablo in a large theatre has not yet been solved.
The nearest approximation to it is undoubtedly that
of the Bristol opera company, which, by sacrificing
the sophisticated ideal of the " puppet-play within
a puppet-play," certainly made the work more directly intelligible, so that its human qualities as well
as its purely musical qualities could and did appeal
immediately to every member of the audience — a
straight and apparently unsophisticated performance
for mixed and apparently unsophisticated spectators.

CHAPTER XI

THE HARPSICHORD CONCERTO

Falla's concerto for harpsichord and small orchestra (which was played in London in June 1927 by the composer and was chosen for performance at the Siena festival in September 1928) shows a further development in the direction of *The Puppet-Show*. It is quite unlike the kind of music which is immediately recognizable as Spanish; yet it leaves us with the paradoxical conviction that the less superficially " Spanish " Falla appears, the more intimately Spanish his music becomes.

Falla is not the first composer who has had to go abroad before he could achieve self-expression. In the sixteenth century Morales and Victoria learnt in Rome how to express themselves like Spaniards; and they did so in a manner which is more intimately Spanish than Guerrero's ever is, although that composer never studied in Italy, but spent the greater part of his life in Seville writing Italianate music. Pedrell, Granados, and Albéniz also went to school abroad. Pedrell, the greatest of the three, was inspired by the example of Wagner — the Wagner of *Die*

Meistersinger — to reveal to Spanish musicians what their musical heritage really was. By insisting on the importance of sixteenth-century music, secular as well as sacred, and by connecting it with folk-song, he did inestimable benefit to Spanish music. Granados discovered the Spanish eighteenth century, the period of Goya, and became the Spanish poet of the pianoforte; while Albéniz turned student again in middle life at the feet of Debussy and created his musical *Iberia* in a sublimation of the sounds of the guitar and the rhythms of the dance. Falla, in addition to all that could be learnt in Paris, has entered into possession of all that he has by birthright in Spain; and that is a musical heritage which is a great deal more extensive, and a great deal more surprising, than many people imagine. It is absurd to suppose, as some French critics and even some Spanish critics would lead us to suppose, that Spain is, musically speaking, a mere colony of Paris.

One of the greatest composers who ever lived in Spain was Domenico Scarlatti; and, considering the years he spent there and the amount of music he wrote, it would be no more unreasonable to describe him as a Spanish composer than it is to describe El Greco as a Spanish painter. In Falla's music, even his earliest published pianoforte pieces, we can feel an intellectual affinity with Scarlatti; and if we try to analyse that feeling, to get it down to some concrete musical fact, we may attribute it largely to his pianoforte technique: the "chopstick" method and the rapidly repeated notes, the wild leaps from one end of the keyboard to the other, the "internal pedals," and (more intimately still) in the rhythms. Yet it does not follow that Falla is necessarily the debtor of Scarlatti in all these things; both may derive them from a common source. The possibility that Scarlatti owed certain of his effects to the Spanish guitar-music of his day has more than once been demonstrated,[1] and it is not unnatural that Falla should sometimes resemble him. Further, the methods and even the material of Scarlatti's music are curiously appropriate to contemporary musical thought. The passion is there, but it is always expressed with concision and clarity; the music is dry and sparkling, but it sparkles in the heat, not in the cold. Scarlatti's music, indeed, glitters like hot Spanish sunshine, illuminating impartially, but not unkindly, tragedy and comedy alike. There can be tragedy leading to despair, as in the incomparable Sonata in B minor; yet even the shadows are hard and clear, not only in outline, and the faintest approach to sentimentality is interrupted by a dry cackle of laughter from across the way. Scarlatti is the exact opposite of Schubert.

Qualities like these, inward as well as outward, must have attracted Falla to Scarlatti, long before he wrote the harpsichord part in *The Puppet-Show* or

[1] *Music and Letters*, April 1922; *Musical Quarterly*, July 1927.

thought of the new concerto; for these Scarlattian qualities are the saving graces of the best contemporary music. What might not have happened to Brahms (I am Northern enough to be able to bear the sound of his name, and even of some of his music, without the familiar, supercilious Latin gesture of disgust), what might not have happened to Brahms if he had come across the Santini MS. of Scarlatti earlier in his life! His pianoforte music might live as long as Chopin's (which ought long ago to have been buried in peace); and, as it is, even Brahms could write passages (for example, in the "*Intermezzo*," Op. 116, no. 4) which, without being a direct imitation, show his mind working in the same way as Scarlatti's.

Falla has been fortunate in the modern revival of the harpsichord. It has been said that he " cannot write for the harpsichord " and that the harpsichord passages in *The Puppet-Show* are ineffective and inaudible. I do not imagine that anyone who has played the part in a performance of *The Puppet-Show* would admit that for a moment! The harpsichord will come through well enough if it is properly placed (in front of the orchestra) and if the strings (which should not exceed the number of performers specified by the composer) are prevented from making too much noise. As to the concerto, it has been alleged that that, too, is not well written for the harpsichord. Falla, after careful experiment with the instrument and prolonged study of the methods of Domenico Scar-

latti, decided what effects he wanted and how they
were to be obtained. It is true that he makes little use
of the endless refinements of the harpsichord, that he
apparently wishes it to be played practically the whole
time with the couplers and that he deliberately avoids
ornaments. What fascinates him is the noble sonority,
the "resounding grace," of the instrument — the
brilliance of a plain scale-passage, the magnificence
of a simple arpeggio, together with the incisive clearness with which a harpsichord invariably speaks.
To say that a man "cannot write" for an instrument because he prefers certain aspects of it is hardly
logical.

The new concerto has an Italian clarity and spa-
ciousness which becomes very noticeable when compared with the bitterly effective *Fantasia Bética,* so
strangely neglected by pianists. The quality common
to both, however, is the quality of directness. Without
preamble Falla dives straight into the midst of the
music; the principal subject comes out with all possible clearness and brilliance, while the strings play
chords on the off beats of the bar.

This apparent simplicity does not last long. Soon, although the clarity and directness are preserved, flute and oboe are found to be playing in one key (B major), and 'cello in another (B flat minor), while the harpsichord plays in A minor in the right hand and B flat minor in the left.

Falla (as far as I can make out) does not believe in "atonality." He would resent an accusation of atonality as he would resent an accusation of atheism, and regards any weakening in tonal feeling — such, for instance, as even Haydn shows in some of his quartets, by the use of "anticipations" — as a weakening of faith. (I do not report the composer as having said this — too many people have reported him as saying things which he never said — but such at any rate is my impression of what he thinks about the question.) Neither in the concerto nor in any other of his works is there any feeling of weakening in tonality. The tonality may be modal, or there may be two or three different tonalities in evidence at the same time; but they are always strongly individualized, contrasted, and distinguished.

The first movement, like the others, is regular enough in form; it has an admirable concision. An episode,

eight bars before No. 14 in the score, has a tune
(given to violin, oboe, and 'cello, spread over four
octaves) which seems to be a reminiscence — though
in a more serious mood — of a gay little tune in *The
Three-Cornered Hat.* It is accompanied on the harpsichord by the first sign of those big arpeggios (played
in opposite directions, up in the right hand, down in
the left) which give such character and such resonance to the whole work.

The slow movement begins with these great
arpeggios, sweeping from one end of the harpsichord
to the other. A suggestion of a canon, with the wind
instruments at their shrillest — the concerto is scored
for flute, oboe, clarinet, violin, and violoncello — is

followed by the culminating point of the whole work, at which the accompanying strings and wind play short, staccato chords, with appoggiaturas in E major; while the harpsichord plays a solemn phrase in arpeggios — "split chords" — in C major.

This is followed by another passage — equally short, but no less forcible — in which the soloist and the accompaniment change places — a suggestion, but only a suggestion, of double counterpoint. The harpsichord repeats a single arpeggio, while the flute, violin, and 'cello have a reminiscence of the theme the harpsichord has just played. Falla may not be able " to write for the harpsichord "; but he has at this moment produced a marvellous climax and a magnificent effect of sound.

The last movement, *Vivace* (*flessibile, scherzando*), is the most Scarlattian of the three, both in

the writing and in the sudden changes from 3/4
to 6/8; it is a movement of unending sparkle and
glitter. The springing opening phrases:

are, as it were, summed up by a passage marked "*con
gioia*":

Another example may show that the composer has, after all, a pretty good notion of how to write for the harpsichord.

In the manuscript copy I have seen, the slow movement is dated: " *A. DOM. MCMXXVI. In Festo Corporis Christi.*" To those who have ever experienced, or imagined, what that festival is like in a Spanish cathedral this movement will certainly give a new meaning to their memories: the confused, magnificent jangle of voices, and instruments, bells, and organ; the subdued grandeur of hanging tapestries and silk brocades, the flare of innumerable candles, and the great silver *custodia,* which enshrines the object of the whole festival. There is not the faintest suggestion of program-music, as there is in Turina's joyous *Procesión del Rocío.* The composer tells me that it was a matter of pure chance that he happened to finish that movement on the morning of Corps. It is merely a vivid pattern in sound and rhythm, but it brings what Albéniz would have called an " *Evocación* " of the most Spanish of all Spanish festivals.

CHAPTER XII

FALLA AND HIS CONTEMPORARIES

I

Some attempt must now be made to show Falla's position in the contemporary musical world and the direction which he is likely to take in the future.

The present state of contemporary music is difficult to describe in a few words and difficult to explain without reference to other contemporary movements. This, however, has already been done by Dr. Hans Mersmann, in " *Die moderne Musik seit der Romantik,*" [1] and by Mr. Percy Scholes in the concluding chapters of *The Listener's History of Music* (Oxford, 1929); so I shall try to treat music independently, avoiding the jargon of the other arts and not applying to music the peculiar isms of contemporary painting or poetry. We hear so much of the opinions of the man of taste, and know so little of the views of the artist, that I should like (in the words of Professor Dent) to be " on the side of the performers," to take music — even contemporary music — as a matter of course and treat it as a thing of everyday life, even

[1] In the *Handbuch der Musikwissenschaft,* edited by Dr. Ernst Bücken (Wildpark-Potsdam, 1929).

though it may be said, as was said of me not long
ago by a contemporary novelist: " You talk about
music as if it were something to *eat!* "

Falla is often credited with aims, opinions, and
ideals which he does not hold, and more often still
emphasis is laid upon " the folk-lore element which
can be discerned in most of de Falla's music, dis-
tinctively national as it is in many of its characteristics." An insignificant detail in this sentence
allows a certain conclusion to be drawn. Falla is not
called " *de* Falla " when the surname is used alone;
such is not the Spanish custom. It follows, therefore,
that the writer of the sentence had his information
at second-hand. As regards the influence of folk-lore
on Falla's music, enough will have been found in the
previous pages to show its real nature and extent.
Falla does not belong to the " folk-song generation,"
still less to the " street-music generation," while his
" orientalism " is due, not to heredity, but to environment. He was a pupil of Pedrell, the most distinguished Spanish representative of the folk-song movement, and a much younger man than Albéniz or
Granados, whose Spanish characteristics are ultimately
derived from street-music.

Reference to an earlier chapter will show that the
term " street-music " is not used as a term of abuse,
but in a sense which is strictly historical. The effects
of street-music on cultivated music have not yet been
fully recognized, nor have the effects of military

march music. The English " quick step," for instance, the 6/8 march tune, seems to have reached Germany in the time of Frederick the Great, and eventually made its way into the work of Beethoven and the other classical composers. Schubert and Weber were much influenced both by military music and by the "military ball-room style," common in Napoleonic times; and Schubert's instrumental works, from the earliest symphonies onwards, show how he was haunted and fascinated by the sound of a military band marching past. Many contemporary composers are haunted in the same way by jazz; and they have as much justification for using it as Schubert had for his *Ländler*.

In the eighteenth century there were distinct types of street-music in Vienna, London, and Madrid. Yet while Viennese street-music has been immortalized by Schubert, and London street-music was the basis of *The Beggar's Opera*, and its sophisticated revivals in the Hammersmith manner, the street-music of eighteenth-century Madrid gave rise to the conventional Spanish musical idiom, which all the world can recognize as Spanish. Viennese street-music and military music have been familiar to us for so long in the works of the classical composers that it is difficult to realize that it is an imported product, if not an exotic one; while *The Beggar's Opera*, an entirely British-made article, seemed new and strange by comparison. In Spain, it is possible that if the truth were known, if

we could ever get into the mind of a Spanish musician and discover what he really felt, we might find
that the suggestion of street-music which hangs about
so much of the classical style is something which still
seems rather commonplace and rather tiresome.
Madrid, perhaps, has never been able to accept the
Viennese school whole-heartedly, just because of this
element of street-music; for at the time when Viennese street-music was exercising its greatest influence
upon the classical composers, Madrid had a very
marked style of street-music of its own (in the *tonadillas*), traces of which are still apparent in the Spanish music of our own time. What the Spanish musician
may be supposed to feel about Vienna, the central-
European musician certainly feels about Spain. When
critics in England have been heard to declare (as we
said before) that they are " tired of the Spanish
idiom "; when French critics find little in Spanish
music but a pleasant form of exoticism, and Germans
dismiss it as *salonmässig* and devoid of that seriousness
which the art of music demands, the reason is that
they are distracted by a certain " street-quality,"
which is foreign to them and which they are unable
either to recognize or to appreciate. This is also the
case with many Spanish musicians, and musicians of
other Latin countries, with regard to the music of
the Viennese school, and probably with regard to the
whole of the classical school as well. This music is
built up on types of melody and types of rhythm

which were either strange to the west-European musical consciousness, or suggested too obviously the music of the military band. And, further, the very fact that classical music is so " built up," on definite " architectural " principles, is, to some Latin peoples, including the Spanish people, strongly against it. Sonata-form, and therefore classical chamber-music, is too indirect and gradual in its expression for some national temperaments. In central Europe, France, and England a composer seems carefully to prepare his ground, so that at last, when his great moment has come and his great announcement is to be made, it shall have an effect enormously increased by all the preparation which has gone before. A Spanish composer, as a rule, works on almost the opposite principle. He will deliver his message straight out, in all its uncompromising force, and subsequent restatements are practically only repetitions driving the point home.

The preceding paragraphs will not, I hope, be taken for an attack on Schubert, or on the whole of classical music. There can be no one, at all sensitive to music, who would not admit that the " Viennese style " and classical chamber-music had provided him with some of his most precious musical experiences. In the same way Professor Einstein would probably admit how precious to him had been the mathematics of Newton; yet that did not prevent him, in dealing with the episode of the falling apple, from seeing that it was not enough to look at it and explain it from Newton's point of view. He had also to consider the point of view of the apple: the branch breaks loose and goes up into the air, while the ground, with Newton sitting on it, rushes up to meet the apple, which, all the time, has remained perfectly still. The methods of relativity are as necessary in music as in physics; we must learn to regard the events of musical history in other " frames of reference " besides our own.

" National characteristics " in music come out in other ways than folk-song and street-music. Nearly every country has its own attitude to music, which differs from that of every other country; and if we are to reject all composers who show any signs of national characteristics, it will deprive us of half the best contemporary music. Stravinsky would have to go (for *Les Noces*), Prokofieff also, Bartók and Kodály, Janáček and all the other Czechs, Vaughan Williams, and Falla. On the other side, the most important nucleus of contemporary composers, the group worth the most serious consideration, is that formed by the Busoni pupils and represented by Jarnach, Křenek, and Kurt Weill, to whom may be added Paul Hindemith, Max Butting, and Wilhelm Maler.

The Schönberg group, on the other hand, seems now to belong definitely to the past. The spirit of pioneering and exploration deserves all the credit and admiration it can attract; but this particular expedition of Schönberg and his followers seems to have ended (like some of the less fortunate expeditions of British or Spanish explorers into unknown regions) in a deep valley from which there is no possible way out. The Andes of contemporary music are still waiting to be climbed; but the Pizarro or Orellana of the future, though he may learn much from the fate of the Schönberg expedition and study its methods, will probably end by taking an entirely different route.

Still more definitely out of date is the "Armistice" school, typified by the French "Six" and so beloved by the directors of the Russian Ballet. Their work was momentarily amusing; but as far as exploration and discovery are concerned, it had about as little to do with pioneering as an expensive and overheated journey in a "Blue Train," and its ideal (if it had one) was a commonplace "Madonna of the Sleeping-Cars."

Composers of individual merit whose national characteristics would be hard to define are to be found in Italy, France, Czecho-Slovakia, Switzerland, Holland, Denmark, Poland, and elsewhere, and especially in the United States. There is also the new school of "neo-classicists" (particularly strong in Italy, where they are led by Casella) who have taken as a model of modern music Stravinsky's *Pulcinella* — a mere arrangement of arias and sonata-movements from Pergolesi, which neither as orchestration nor as music can be compared for a moment with the exquisite

Scarlatti pieces, arranged by Tommasini for the ballet of *The Good-humoured Ladies*. This so-called neo-classic movement — so different from the constructive neo-classic ideal upheld by Busoni — has broken out in various forms: in England and France and to a certain extent in Germany also it is " back to Bach," in Italy " back to Vivaldi," while with Stravinsky it has now taken the form of " back to Tschaikovsky." These movements are in no sense an advance; still less are they exploration. They are the movements, not of pioneers, but of tourists, who ascend well-known peaks by well-worn tracks, or even by a funicular railway. They get a view, of course, but they see it through the eyes of others.

Compared with the sterility of such movements, the folk-song movement was fertilizing indeed, and might have had far greater effects if it had not been for the European war. At the present time there is a remarkable difference between the attitude of central Europe towards all folk-song and primitive music and that of eastern Europe or western. Paris, though the French folk-song style (as represented by Paul Ladmirault, for instance, or Guy Ropartz) has never made any great impression on it, has always been ready to toy with the " exotic " in music; yet Debussy was almost the only composer who ever took it seriously. The Germans, on the contrary, have a strange if not altogether unaccountable fear of " barbarian " music. After all, from whatever " frame of reference " we regard it — English, French, or Spanish — the German musical tradition is the most solid achievement of civilized music in existence; and if with that we combine the Italian tradition, as it was combined in Lasso, Bach, Handel, Mozart, and Busoni, we find some of the greatest and most permanent values in European music. This great German-Italian tradition is not lightly to be put aside, and it is no wonder that even the youngest and most adventurous of contemporary German composers, however thoroughly they may have turned their backs on the German nineteenth century, are somewhat shy of all new music bearing a national stamp (or, as Stravinsky would say, a " passport ") which is not central European. Music from Hungary, Czecho-Slovakia, Russia, Spain, produces a feeling of something like fear on German minds; and French music when it is not merely frivolous *Unterhaltungsmusik,* so far from being " the Defence of the West," has (it is sometimes believed in Germany) actually let the enemy in; so that civilized European music (that is to say, German music) is now surrounded and threatened by the music of the barbarians. England alone seems to have, for alert German musicians, a national music which they can understand, since the modern English " national style " (as represented by Vaughan Williams) can be related quite definitely to the music of the time of Shakspere and therefore cannot possibly be considered as " barbarian."

An English musician, " born Teuton and bred Latin," as it has been said, will be able to see things from both sides, in both " frames of reference." He will sympathize with the German point of view without necessarily sharing it; and he will be able to see that there is something of immense value in the music of the " barbarians " which is not merely " exotic." He may even be able to understand the German attitude, which, unwilling or unable to take " barbarian " music altogether seriously, is inclined to dismiss it as *salonmässig,* fit for a drawing-room entertainment rather than for a concert room, a temple of the art of music. This is perhaps a stage better than the conventional French attitude, inclined to regard all such music as a curious object for a Paris exhibition, rather than as the normal musical expression of a people with different musical traditions from their own. Yet to consider Spanish or Hungarian music as a drawing-room entertainment is almost equally wide of the mark. We have all read of the orgies at which Hungarian music is performed in its own country; while in Spain the *cante hondo,* which has been the inspiration of some of the best work of Falla, belongs (as we have seen) to places as remote from a drawing-room as anything in Europe, being the music (or what was once the music) of the depths of existence — of vagabonds, prisons, and brothels. To anyone possessed of the characteristically Spanish sense of humour it must be distinctly amusing to learn that what was known to be, or to have been originally, the music of the lowest of low life was considered by many musicians to be romantic music, eminently suitable for a drawing-room! The consequence, however, is unfortunate, for it leads to the work of the greatest living Spanish composer being seriously underestimated in the country of the greatest musical tradition. Falla, in his most recent works, hardly sounds " Spanish " at all; even in Paris *The Puppet-Show* was a puzzle to the critics, because it did not sound in the least as Spanish music is fashionably supposed to sound. The same might be said of Bartók and Kodály. They cannot be dismissed as mere folk-lore composers and " barbarian " musicians because they have been influenced by the rhythmic and melodic formulæ of folk-music and by the characteristic accentuation of their native speech. On the contrary, they, with Stravinsky and the Russians who preceded him, and with the Czecho-Slovak jazz composers as well, have brought something new into Western music — something to be absorbed or rejected, a toxin (if you like) which may in time produce its own antitoxin for the general health of civilized music.

After all, it is no use grumbling at folk-music and resenting its intrusion. By studying it, and the history of art-music as well, we find that the conditions of today have occurred before at various periods of musical history; that folk-music is always there, outside the door, and has always been ready to come in for a little whenever the door was opened. The door is ajar once more. To say nothing of the " folk-song movement " which belongs to the period before the war when the door seemed to be open more widely than it is at present, the annual festivals of the International Society for Contemporary Music have shown that there are other ways in which music influenced by folk-lore is getting in, and bringing new ideas and new methods within the reach of contemporary composers. This is especially true with regard to choral works. Kodály's *Psalmus Hungaricus* has been frequently performed in England since its introduction to an international gathering of musicians at the Zürich festival of 1926, while two remarkable Jugo-Slav works have also been performed by the society: Petyrek's *Litany* and Širola's unaccompanied oratorio *The Life and Works of SS. Cyril and Methodius*. An oratorio, and, above all, an oratorio with so paralysing a title as *The Life and Works* of two somewhat exotic saints, might seem enough to frighten away anyone whose chief interest was in the adventurous music of pioneer composers. Yet those among the audience at Frankfurt who endured to the end — who risked being late for the Burgomaster's luncheon and missing the superb wines of the Saar from the municipal cellars — were rewarded by a musical experience which they will not easily forget: one of those strange thrills which do not come every day or even every year to those in the habit of listening to music.

There are other ways in which folk-music, or primitive music, is getting in. The chief of these is by " quarter tones "; while another most interesting experiment was the " Voice-band " directed by E. F. Burian, another Czech composer. The musical effect of this would be difficult to describe, but it certainly suggested primitive music in the use of intervals not to be obtained from the tempered scale of the piano-forte. Whatever theoretical objections there may be to the employment of quarter tones in harmony, on the pianoforte, as Alois Hába uses them, it cannot be denied that he is doing good work in the cause of experimental music, and his two- and three-part counterpoint in quarter tones is a new and thrilling experience. Hába has found a pianoforte-maker willing to construct an experimental instrument with two keyboards — that is to say, two complete pianos in one — tuned a quarter of a tone apart. The experiment has not yet wholly succeeded, for the sound is more like that of a lodging-house piano than anything else. The new intervals, when the notes are struck simultaneously, sound dull in the bass; and in the treble — anywhere above the middle C — they are detestable. Owing to the bad effect of the overtones, the quality of tone is peculiarly thin and " cracked," like that of an ordinary piano out of tune — a defect which in the future it may be possible to remedy, unless indeed Hába positively enjoys these sounds, as being yet one more protest against romanticism and

Gefühlsduselei. Busoni had a theory of music in thirds of a tone, not quarter tones, and a harmonium was made for him which is said not to have suffered from these defects; indeed, to a pianist with so exquisite an ear for the beauty of pianoforte tone as Busoni had, the noises produced by Hába's quarter-tone piano would have been excruciating.

The real trouble lies in the nature of quarter tones, and the way they are used in primitive music, or in civilized music like that of India. It is not correct to say that they cannot be used in harmony. They *are* so used, in vocal music of the madrigal period, for the performance of which it is essential to sharpen or flatten certain notes and certain intervals in order to make the passage sound in tune. They are also used in such civilized music as a Brahms string-quartet, where, now and again, experienced players almost unconsciously sharpen or flatten certain notes for the same reason. In folk-music, however, where there is no harmony, quarter tones (or, rather, intervals sharper or flatter than can be played on the pianoforte) are used as a means of expression. To give point to a certain note in the phrase, or to a certain word in the line, a note will be unexpectedly sharpened or flattened; and a real singer of folk-songs (like Madame Geni Sadero) will pitch that note in exactly the same place every time the phrase recurs, showing that it was not an accident, and that the singer was not unconsciously singing out of tune. The last time I was at Granada, there was a muleteer who passed the house singing, every morning, and pitched his odd intervals absolutely true every time, occasionally interrupting his song with a cry of *arrí* to his beast — which was presumably as interested in the quarter tones as I was, and, like me, had stopped to listen. That cry, and a distant bell somewhere, seemed to be the only possible sort of accompaniment to the song.

The use of folk-song in cultivated music does not necessarily mean a lack of melodic invention in the composer who uses it; on the contrary, it often shows that the composer is more than usually sensitive to melody. But it must be deprived of all its drawing-room suggestions. It must also lose its suggestions of terror, of barbarism. It has enriched art-music before now, and may do so again. How this will come about will be discovered by the adventurous pioneer composers. It may be by freer rhythms (which we have already begun to enjoy in modern music), or by the use of unusual intervals (the so-called "quarter tones") or by the grace-notes, turns, and trills which the unaccompanied singer of folk-songs uses as a means of expression or as a substitute for harmony. Alois Hába is trying to systematize these strange intervals on his quarter-tone piano; and that, if used as a melodic rather than a harmonic instrument, may help us to grow accustomed to them and to train our ears to hearing them. But, above all, we shall have to train singers to make these fine intervals; and that will only be accomplished when they have learnt to be as accurate and steady in their intonation, as honest and straightforward in their intention, as Geni Sadero.

II

Falla's music first became widely known during the critical years after the Armistice. The supply of music, west of the Rhine, had temporarily failed; and instead of music there were the inanities of one, the pleasant fooling of another, and the circus style of a third. Music, it was said, must be kept " pure " and " Latin "; there must be no poison from across the Rhine. The word seems to have gone round that the style of these composers was " the thing "; and intellectual snobbery did its best to see that it was firmly established.

The eccentricities of this group drove many composers into frank reaction against any kind of modern music. In their student days before the war they had amused one another by playing Haydn minuets with the treble in one key and the bass in another; now they saw this sort of thing printed, published, and performed as serious music. It is possible to think of composers in England who might have written interesting or even great music, if they had not been frightened away from the musical expression of their own time by the clowns in Paris, and had had enough historical perspective to realize that the " Armistice " style was merely a passing mood — the mood of a number of people who have unexpectedly won a lottery and then discover that their debts and income tax will cost them more than the lottery is worth. The " Armistice " style depended to a certain extent on guying the composers of the romantic period; but when, these being exhausted, the " Armistice " musicians turned to Bach, they found that John Sebastian was not a composer who could be guyed. He might be imitated, it was true, in some of his more obvious expressions; and these imitations (though they had about as much to do with the soul of Bach as with his wig) began to attract the attention of the older composers once more. Here at last was modern music which they could understand, and which was obviously far inferior to the old! The young composers might produce a tolerable imitation of Bach's " busy " counterpoint, but they could never write a Bach slow movement.

Meanwhile the idea began to gain ground in Italy that modern music must be taught to behave itself; and a new style was evolved, based upon Stravinsky's *Pulcinella*. This work had considerable influence in western Europe during the period immediately following the Armistice: but its consequences (in the opinion of the present writer, at any rate) were hardly fortunate for west-European music. To come down from the splendid adventures of *Pétrouchka*, *Les Noces*, and *Le Sacre* to the smooth and easy path of re-arranging other people's music was a disappointing end to the career of an intrepid explorer. The change of style was all the more regrettable in a composer whose sincerity had been recognized even before the war, and only began to be doubted after the Armistice, when ardent propagandists of " Latin " music endeavoured to associate Stravinsky with themselves. The truth was that west-European music, especially that portion of it produced between the Rhine and the Pyrenees, seemed likely to die of inanition, cut off as it was from central and northern Europe, from young Germany, Busoni and Sibelius.

Falla arrived at exactly the right moment. If *The Three-Cornered Hat* saved the musical reputation of the Russian Ballet, the *Nights in the Gardens of Spain* showed that modern music had still something new and thrilling to say and was not all pure foolery. *El Amor Brujo* was new in a recognizably Spanish style, while *The Puppet-Show* and the Harpsichord Concerto broke new ground by showing that a Spanish composer could cease to be obviously and recognizably Spanish and yet hold the attention of the whole of musical Europe. Falla's music (as has been already pointed out) gave everyone the chance of becoming acquainted with the tendencies of serious contemporary composers. His methods sometimes reminded the audience of Stravinsky, Bartók, or Vaughan Williams; but they seemed to be more immediately accessible, while the boldness of his design

and the vigour of his execution never left his meaning
in doubt. With Falla, harmony has become less
important as a means of giving " perspective " to a
piece of music, of allowing it to be seen " in the
round." Modulation is reduced to a minimum. The
chief means of expression are melody and rhythm:
the former consisting of short, incisive phrases presented with the contrasted and unblended colours
of various instruments (wind, percussion, and strings
plucked rather than bowed); while the latter depends
upon the clearness of accent and cross-accent, so that
a vital combination of conflicting rhythms becomes
a guiding principle of the whole work. Lastly, there
is no suggestion of improvisation, romantic hesitation,
or feeling the way; the interpreter does not come
before us and let his fingers wander " idly over the
noisy keys " until the divine inspiration falls upon
him. With Falla, we feel that the music has already
been going on for some time elsewhere, when the performer by art or magic begins to let us hear it.

The preceding chapters have endeavoured to
show something of the course of Falla's development
from *La Vida Breve* through the *Nights in the Gardens of Spain*, *El Amor Brujo*, *The Three-Cornered
Hat*, and the *Fantasia Bética*, to *The Puppet-Show*
and the Harpsichord Concerto. These with the *Three
Songs to words by Théophile Gautier*, the *Quatre
Pièces pour le piano*, *Seven Spanish Songs*, the *Homenaje* for guitar, on the death of Claude Debussy,

Psyche (for voice and five instruments), and the *Soñnet of Góngora* represent the whole of his published work. It is a short list, but it contains no potboilers; every bar has been written and rewritten until the composer was satisfied with it, and *El Amor Brujo* and *The Three-Cornered Hat* were originally performed in versions different from those which were afterwards printed.

A few pages earlier (p. 169), reference was made to new and adventurous choral works by contemporary composers: Kodály's *Psalmus Hungaricus*, Petyrek's *Litany*, and Širola's *Life and Works of SS. Cyril and Methodius*; while a new choral work as adventurous as any, though not hitherto performed outside Great Britain, is the *Sancta Civitas* of Vaughan Williams.

The new work on which Falla is at present engaged is also a choral work: *Atlántida*. It is based on the epic by Jacinto Verdaguer, and the greater part of the text which the composer has chosen for setting to music is taken from the poem itself, in its original language, which is not ordinary Spanish, but Catalan —the language of Barcelona and the north-eastern Spanish provinces on the Mediterranean coast.

The story which the work tells is the story of the lost country of Atlantis, sunk in the sea beyond the western coast of Spain. "Do you see that great ocean?" the chorus asks, seeing in imagination the Pillars of Hercules and the Atlantic Ocean beyond.

" In other times that was the Garden of the Hesperides. Here the Titans strove; cities flourished. Everywhere were the songs of maidens and the music of birds. Now in the marble palaces the seals are gathered and the lawns are clothed with sea-weed." The work goes on to tell of the last labours of Hercules: how he killed Geryon, king of Cadiz, and slew the dragon which guarded the golden apples of the Hesperides. He broke open the Straits of Gibraltar, and the waves rushed over the doomed Atlantis. The Titans climbed the highest mountain in the land and built a tower there which almost reached the sky; but they were cast into the depths of the sea, and their sepulchre is marked by Mount Teide, the volcano of Tenerife. There remain the white blossoms of the Hesperian tree, planted by Hercules at Cadiz, and the golden apples, which have grown once more in the gardens of Spain, while the seven Hesperides have been changed into stars; but that is all that is left of the lost land of Atlantis, which sank beneath the sea.

At the words of the chorus we see a new world rising before us in imagination. The story gives wings to the thought of navigators and explorers. Christopher Columbus, offers to go out and discover the New World. Genoa, Venice, and Portugal refuse to support him, but Isabella of Castile dreams of what may come, and sells her jewels to help the expedition. From a promontory we watch the departure of the three little ships on the greatest of all adventures; and to the eyes of Columbus the palm-trees of the first sighted land grow into a vast building filled with music.

That, in broad outline, is the subject of Falla's *Atlántida*. Not all of these events may appear in the finished work, but this is the background of the thought. It is a great subject, and one worthy of a composer who has never been backward in exploring the untrodden ways of music.

APPENDIX

The following rough translations of the *Seven Spanish Songs* have been made to fit the music exactly and may be sung if necessary instead of the Spanish. They should not be considered apart from the music.

1

That Moorish cloth in the window,
The finest cloth in the window —
A stain had fallen upon it,
Some foul stain had fallen upon it.

'Twas sold for less in the market,
The price was low in the market;
For half its value had gone;
Yes, half its value had gone.

2

Now all good people hear me
That have glass houses!
Now all good people that have glass houses
(Hear you, that have glass houses!),
Look that you never throw more stones
And hit your neighbour's!
For we're both drovers,

And maybe in a lonely road
(It may be in a lonely road!)
   We meet one evening.

With your uncommon faithlessness
  There's no comparing.
There's no comparing — unless it be a sixpence
  (A silver sixpence!),
That's current coin in all the land
  And been in all men's hands;
  Until 'tis rubbed so smooth
That all think it's a bad one;
And if it be a bad one,
No man will take it.
   (Nobody take it!)

3

When I longed for relief from my pain,
I lay down by a pine-tree so green;
When I longed for relief from my pain.

Then it knew that I wept, and wept too;
And that pine-tree whose leaves were so green,
When it knew that I wept, it wept too.

4

All the village says we've quarrelled
(They're all sure we must have quarrelled!),
  While we never speak a word;

Let them ask your heart and my heart
   (Ask both hearts of ours and welcome).
All the village says we've quarrelled,
   While we never speak a word.

Now I say good-bye to you
   (Time to say good-bye to you!).
   Leave your house and leave your window.
Though your mother hate to hear me,
Good-night, sweet, until tomorrow;
So good-night, my dear, till morning.
Leave your house and leave you too.
(But your mother hates to hear me!)

5

Lullaby, lullay, lullay,
   Bye-bye, my baby;
Lullaby, little morning star,
   Bye-bye, my baby.

Lullay, lullay, now,
   Bye-bye, my baby;
Sleep, my star of the morning,
   Bye-bye, my baby.

6

Those eyes of yours were traitors!
So will I treat them.

Those eyes of yours deceivers!
So will I meet them.
You know not what it cost me,
La la la,
Gazing upon them,
La la, la la la,
Gazing upon them,
La la.

Love's lost (they say) between us;
But you were mine once!
All's past (they say) between us;
For you were mine once!
Something is counted gain, then!
La la la,
Something was lost too!
La la, la la la,
Something was lost, then!
La la.

7

Oh my heart — ah!
Broken heart — ah!
Heart that's rent with pain and torment,
Seared and rent with pain and torment,
Ah!
And no man must know at all!

A curse be on love — accursèd!
May God curse this love — accursèd!
Ah!
And a curse on her as well!

INDEX

i

INDEX

A

NOTE

ON THE

TYPE IN

WHICH THIS

BOOK IS SET

*This book is set on
the Linotype in Gara-
mond, a modern rendering
of the type first cut in
the sixteenth century by Claude
Garamont (1510–1561). He was
a pupil of Geofroy Tory and is
believed to have based his letters on
Venetian models, although he introduced
a number of important differences. It is to
him we owe the letter which we know as Old Style.*

COMPOSED BY THE PLIMPTON PRESS, NORWOOD,
MASS. PRINTED AND BOUND BY H. WOLFF ESTATE,
NEW YORK. PAPER MADE BY S. D. WARREN CO., BOSTON.